The American GI Forum

The American GI Forum

In Pursuit of the Dream, 1948-1983

Henry A. J. Ramos

Foreword by Raul Yzaguirre

Arte Público Press
Houston, Texas
1998

This volume is made possible through grants from the Ford Foundation and the City of Houston through The Cultural Arts Council of Houston, Harris County.

Recovering the past, creating the future

Arte Público Press
University of Houston
Houston, Texas 77204-2090

E
184
.M5
R33
1998

Ramos, Henry A. J.
 The American GI Forum: in pursuit of the dream, 1948-1983 / by Henry Ramos.
  p.   cm.
  ISBN 1-55885-261-1   (alk. paper) — ISBN 1-55885-262-X (trade paper : alk. paper)
  1. American G.I. Forum — History. 2. Mexican Americans — Civil rights — History — 20th century. 3. Mexican Americans — Societies, etc. — History — 20th century. 4. Hispanic Americans — Civil rights—History — 20th century. 5. Hispanic americans — Societies, etc.—History — 20th century. 6. Hispanic American veterans — Societies, etc. — History — 20th century. I. Title.
E184.M5R33   1998
323.1'16872073'06073—dc21   98-8679
                                                                          CIP

♾ The paper used in this publication meets the requirements of the American National Standard for Information Sciences—Permanence of Paper for Printed Library Materials, ANSI Z39.48-1984.

8 9 0 1 2 3 4 5 6 7   10 9 8 7 6 5 4 3 2 1

Contents

Illustrations

Foreword

As a young man growing up in south Texas during the 1950s, I vividly remember the conditions that gave rise to the formation of the American GI Forum. For Mexican Americans in south Texas and the Rio Grande Valley (the birthplace of the Forum and numerous other leading national Hispanic organizations), life was hard. Opportunities for Hispanics to acquire meaningful employment and schooling were limited by law and local custom. Housing and health conditions were dangerously substandard, and local Anglo service establishments, from restaurants and hotels to hospitals and barber shops, were frequently off-limits to Latinos. Much like blacks in the South, Hispanic Americans in Texas and much of the nation were denied equal treatment under the law as a matter of course.

After World War II, returning Hispanic servicemen and women found these conditions intolerable. They organized and fought for change. The American GI Forum became their primary vehicle to advance this work. For younger Hispanics of the day like myself, the Forum's early activities and successes established a first exposure to the possibility of equality. The Forum's work exposed us to the critical importance of patriotism, community organization, education, advocacy, and leadership. It helped to focus us on a purpose in our lives larger than just ourselves. It gave us—sometimes for the first time—pride in our history and our contributions to American society and culture.

I remember, as a youth leader of the organization, the opportunity to meet and work with the Forum's founding leaders, including Dr. Hector P. García. They taught me the value of dedication and hard work as I helped to organize youth chapters of the group, first in Texas and then in other states. These early Forum leaders, and García in particular, were my first heroes. They were selfless, tireless workers. They had a vision. Yet they were entirely human. Most were quite humble, and few seemed to comprehend that their efforts were helping to revolutionize America's relationship to Hispanics and other minority people.

Only those who actually lived during the Forum's early years can fully appreciate how risky the organization's work was. In a moment of deep national sentiment against foreign people, at the height of the excesses of the McCarthy era, and in some of the most viscerally racist communities in America, the GI Forum's agenda was inherently provocative. Frequently, the Forum's work was met with resistance. But the organization's base veterans and their families, its staunch commitment to established American ideals, and its successful employment of patriotic symbols and religious rituals all helped to establish some political space for Hispanic activism. In many cases and in many communities, the Forum was the only viable community mechanism through which meaningful change could be advocated without mainstream rejection or even violent reprisal.

Indeed, the GI Forum's early contributions to national Hispanic civil rights and community identity were seminal. The Forum, often in conjunction with the League of United Latin American Citizens (LULAC), pioneered the first Hispanic civil-rights cases in the nation's highest courts. It was the first such organization to successfully challenge local and state-supported segregation of Hispanic public school students. It was also the first Hispanic organization to do serious business with national elected and appointed officials, and the first such group to effectively lobby for programs for the special needs of Spanish-speaking Americans. The Forum's organizing practices and agenda established the standards and foundations upon which all subsequent significant Hispanic groups have built: The National Council of La Raza, The Mexican American Legal Defense and Educational Fund, and the Southwest Voter Registration and Education Project, and others.

Today, unfortunately, it is frequently the case that the GI Forum's many contributions to American society and culture are not fully appreciated. Particularly among younger Americans, Hispanic and non-Hispanic alike, the Forum's history has been largely forgotten.

School programs and the public media, until recently, have failed to emphasize Hispanic contributions to American civic culture. And those institutions and programs that have provided insight into Hispanic experiences in America have tended to focus only on more recent activities, absent coverage of the foundational work for these undertakings.

The American GI Forum: In Pursuit of the Dream, 1948-1983 provides timely and important insights into the GI Forum's development. Arriving on the occasion of the Forum's fifty-year anniversary, at a time of renewed discussion of issues such as immigration, bilingual education, and affirmative action, the book reminds us that America's civil-rights struggle continues. At the same time, it underscores the many valuable lessons the Forum taught us in its formative years related to the value of sustained community engagement, mobilization, spirit, and tenacity. With all of the challenges Hispanics face in America today, there was a time, as this work reminds us, when conditions were worse: when merely being Hispanic definitively disqualified an individual from meaningful social and economic advancement; when being dark-skinned and Spanish-surnamed qualitatively dismissed one's convictions and opinions in public discussion and debate; when being Hispanic diminished or nullified one's legal rights. We are grateful to have made progress since those painful times that marked the GI Forum's emergence, making way for what has become the contemporary Hispanic civil-rights movement. Our challenges, though still formidable, are far more palatable than fifty years ago; our opportunities to positively shape our place in and contributions to U. S. society far greater. To this we owe the American GI Forum a great deal.

I strongly encourage readers of this book to carefully consider its contents, to reflect deeply on their implications, and to share its insights with family, friends, and colleagues. It is in the nature of our responsibility to one another, as members of the American family, to share stories in this vein so that they will never be forgotten. Only in this way will America and its Hispanic people ever truly realize the American dream that is at the heart of the GI Forum's origins, motivations, and accomplishments.

Raul Yzaguirre
Washington, D. C.
July, 1998

Acknowledgments

No book is the product of one individual's work alone, particularly if it highlights a subject as colorful as the history of the American GI Forum. I have *many* people to thank and acknowledge for their assistance with and contributions to the story that follows. Interviews conducted in the field and over the telephone were essential to the completion of this work. I am indebted to all those who gave so graciously of their time, insight, and assistance.

The staffs of the American GI Forum's National Historical Foundation and Archives, and of Dr. Hector P. García's medical offices, were exceptionally hospitable during my original field research in Corpus Christi, Texas; to these people I owe special thanks. Several long-standing Forumeers provided invaluable and telling information about the Forum's early growth and later development. These individuals include Sonny Saavedra, the late Bernie Sandoval, Rosa Ena Guitiérrez, Dr. Xico García, and Dr. Clotilde García, of Corpus Christi, Texas; Dominga Coronado, of New Braunfels, Texas; Carlos Martínez, of San Antonio, Texas; Louis and Isabelle Téllez, of Albuquerque, New Mexico; and Jake Alarid, of Los Angeles, California.

I am particularly grateful for the time, feedback, and assistance provided by several distinguished friends and observers of the Forum, including Albert Camarillo and John Gardner, of Palo Alto, California; Sandy Close and Herman Gallegos, of San Francisco, California; Bert Corona, of Los Angeles, California; Victor Becerra of Phoenix, Arizona; Polly Baca Barragán, of Denver, Colorado; Vicente Ximenes, of Albuquerque, New Mexico; Dr. Tom Krenek and Grace Charles of Corpus Christi, Texas; and Raúl Yzaguirre, of Washington, D. C.

Additionally I extend appreciation to Carl Allsup, whose book *The American GI Forum: Origins and Evolution*[1] is an authoritative first work on the organization's foundations. I have drawn heavily from his insightful analysis, as well as his early encouragement to complete this work as a means of expanding the base of public information on the Forum's many contributions to U. S. society.[2]

John Tucker, formerly of the American Gas Association, and Santana González of Chevron USA also warrant special mention. Their efforts were instrumental in securing the initial funding required to complete this text's first publication in 1983 as a GI Forum monograph covering the period 1948-1972. Although the present publication offers significantly more in-depth treatment of the subject matter, it fundamentally builds on research and writing incorporated in the monograph.

The present work—and its national distribution to schools, libraries, and nonprofit community groups—is made possible by Anthony Romero of the Ford Foundation, whose generous financial support and enduring commitment to social justice causes will always serve as an inspiration to me. In addition, I am extremely grateful to Dr. Nicolas Kanellos and Arte Público Press at the University of Houston for their support and assistance.

Deepest appreciation is extended to Gilbert Chávez, formerly of the U. S. Department of Education (USDE), and to the late José Cano, national chairman of the American GI Forum during 1980-1983. Without them I would never have been afforded the opportunity to work on this important project. Chávez introduced me to Cano in 1980, during my tenure as a University of California "Cal in the Capitol" intern in USDE's Office of Hispanic Concerns. Cano, who hired me to be his special assistant when he became Forum national chairman later that year, conceived the idea of producing an official GI Forum history in monograph form and oversaw its completion. He was a tough-minded and unusually determined leader who almost always accomplished what he set out to do. He taught me and others a great deal about politics and American society. It was a sad day when he passed away in 1988, following a protracted battle with diabetes. He was only 47 years old. I know José would be pleased to see this work published.

Another individual to whom I am especially grateful is the man who *truly* made this book a possibility—the late Dr. Hector P. Garciá, who founded the American GI Forum. During the fall of 1981, I spent a week with the doctor in Corpus Christi recording his thoughts and recollections in preparation of this work's original manuscript. His kindness, compassion, and vision made him a model civic leader for nearly fifty years; and my appreciation of his accomplishments and friendship, always profound, has grown over time. In July 1996, the doctor succumbed to pneumonia and heart failure at age 84. I am, as others who knew García, fortunate to have been touched by him. He was a remarkable human being.

Especially deserving of recognition as well are various members of Dr. García's immediate family, whose encouragement and support of my efforts to have this book published were extremely important. Wanda Fusillo García, the doctor's widow, her daughters Wanda and Cecilia, and Cecilia's husband, Jim Akers, all warrant special mention. I consider them all good friends and among the kindest people I met on my journey to complete this book.

There are many more thousands of individuals to whom I must apologize for not being able to recount their particular contributions to the Forum's growth and development. Here, I am thinking of the rank and file members of the American GI Forum. Clearly, their importance to the Forum's evolution and to the contents of this book cannot be overstated. While I have not been able here to cite each of their important stories and experiences, I hope those among them who have occasion to read this book will at least take pride and solace from having been such an integral part of the Forum's impressive history.

Finally, it is important to acknowledge the support and inspiration of various colleagues, friends and loved ones, without whom I could never successfully have completed this work. Pamela Goldschmidt, Antonio Manning, Bonnie Kirk, Jojo Kwok, and Heather Wiedmeyer deserve accolades for tolerating me, and then helping me, through key stages of the book's conceptual and editorial development. My grandparents—Josephine Ramos, and Jesse and Carmen Rodríguez—all now deceased, warrant special recognition for having inspired during my childhood a strong pride and interest in Mexican-American history, including the critical work of groups like the GI Forum. Last, but certainly not least, my loving wife, Claudia Lenschen-Ramos, provided unending help, encouragement, and affirmation as I completed this long-standing project. To her, as always, I am most indebted.

Henry A. J. Ramos
Berkeley, California

Introduction

Throughout American history, countless writers, thinkers, and communities have idealized and promoted the concept of the American dream. Though often using different terminology, advocates of the concept have resonated to certain shared beliefs. In the nineteenth century the quasi-religious term *manifest destiny* emerged to describe important aspects of the dream. Its development suggested a strong sense of America as a uniquely good, just, and free nation; it also invoked a certain assurance of America's inevitable expansion and greatness.

Shortly after the turn of the century, Herbert Croly wrote of *The Promise of American Life.* The promise, according to Croly, was built on the imaginative projection of a national ideal "with wonderful and more than national possibilities."[1] It was based on a belief that somehow and sometime, something better would happen to good Americans than had happened to the people of any other country.

Richard Hofstader went beyond these concepts to describe in his 1948 work *The American Political Tradition* the staple tenets of American civic culture.[2] These included the value of opportunity and the "natural evolution of individual self-interest and self-assertion, within broad legal limits, into a beneficent social order." According to Hofstader, all of this strongly biased Americans to favor egalitarian democracy.

In the early 1960s, drawing on these streams of thought, the great spiritual and political leader Dr. Martin Luther King, Jr., stirred national passions with his famous "I Have a Dream" speech, at the foot of the Lincoln Memorial. King's vision of an America in which individuals would be judged not by the color of their skin, but rather by the content of their character, provoked a fundamental reconfiguration of the nation's social standards and moral foundations. In effect, King extended the dream's reach to previously unincorporated segments of the American community.

While these outlooks vary in semantics and focus, they point to recurrent themes that broadly define the American dream—freedom, democracy, justice, equality, opportunity, morality, destiny. That the dream lacks a more specific or more cogent definition does not negate its far-reaching historical and cultural impact. In fact, while we in America never have developed a collective definition of the American dream, few would deny that historically Americans have adhered to at least personalized notions of the concept and its significance. For most this has included a firm conviction in the inevitability of socioeconomic opportunity and mobility in one's own lifetime, and in one's own family through the generations. This in turn has translated into a broadly shared belief in the sanctity of individual talents and pursuits, and the basic right to expand one's own life possibilities in a free and growing society and economy. Inherently and increasingly related to this have been fundamental guarantees of individual and political rights not afforded in other nations.

Whatever the real-life inconsistencies or contradictions of these notions, conviction in the dream's essential foundations developed through the twentieth century as a real and pervasive component of the American identity. In practice, this afforded American leaders extraordinary wherewithal and much-needed legitimacy to confront and overcome increasingly complex domestic and world crises. With America's triumphs over the Great Depression of the 1930s and the Axis powers in the Second World War, thereafter, the American dream gained its most fervent and widespread subscription.

Among the millions of American soldiers returning to civilian life after World War II were tens of thousands of Mexican descent eager to immerse themselves in the American dream their victories overseas had helped preserve. As individuals and as a people these men had distinguished themselves in battle.[3] In Europe, in North Africa, and in the Pacific, American soldiers of Mexican origin fought courageously. When necessary they gave their lives. Many were awarded congressional medals of honor, distinguished service crosses, and silver and bronze stars for their demonstrated valor in combat.[4] These men had played an integral role in the Allied victory that made the United States the world's most powerful nation. In their hearts and minds they knew this, and it changed their entire outlook and perspective. Indeed their return to America was marked by intense optimism in the democratic future their own actions had shaped and made possible.

Unfortunately, but in retrospect not surprisingly, the spirit Mexican-American soldiers carried back with them from overseas was unmatched by the society to which they returned. There, little had changed since the pre-war period, which for Mexican Americans had been marked by over one hundred years of second-class citizenship beneath a dominant Anglo power structure. Mexican-American servicemen returned to find themselves and their families confronted with the same biases and indignities they had experienced before the war. Typically, Mexican Americans were subjected to degrading public slurs: "greaser," "pepper belly," "meskin." In many places, restaurant and restroom signs read, "No Dogs or Mexicans Allowed."[5] Mainstream sentiments along these lines constrained Mexican Americans from fully accessing the employment, educational, and housing opportunities of the day. And while Anglo veterans around the nation re-entered the mainstream of civilian life with relative smoothness via expedited GI Bill assistance, Mexican-American veterans somehow found their entitlements delayed or woefully insufficient upon receipt.

Practically overnight, these demonstrably valiant guardians of the American dream were forgotten, resigned by the powers that be to a place all too familiar in their past but no longer possible or acceptable for their future. Rather, these veterans stood prepared to struggle as never before for their rightful place as citizens of the United States of America. They had courageously defended the nation in battle for this right and they expected, as did Americans of other backgrounds, the full benefits attendant to their citizenship.

Mexican-American claims to these benefits went beyond the scope of the GI Bill; they went instead to the very heart of the American dream, touching all aspects of American life. Increasingly, Mexican Americans were becoming aware that many impediments to their opportunity and mobility in American society were embedded in institutional policies that built prejudice and inequality into the American system. Their response was not radical, as might be expected, but it was revolutionary in a most American way.

From town to town, from city to city, and from state to state they built themselves an organization, an institution of their very own. With pride and resolve they named their organization the American GI Forum, connoting their belief in democratic American principles. They built their organization from the ground up through faith in American ideals and pride in the role persons of their ancestry, religious belief, and family commitment had played, and would continue to play, in upholding those ideals. These were the traditional sources of apprehension and prejudice towards Mexican Americans outside their own communities—ethnicity, Catholicism, and extended family networks. But within their communities they were indomitable sources of will and strength.

In cars owned or borrowed, on weekends or vacation time, Forumeers would travel together: families and friends, mile after mile, spreading the word of their organization. They were predominantly representative of the lower and working classes of their communities, people of limited educational skills and financial resources but unlimited commitment and drive. In the absence of material wealth, they pooled what little resources they had as a group to support their many endeavors. They operated on sheer faith and conviction in their organizational objectives. To their own people, and to the public at large, they emphasized and reemphasized the organization's patriotic, familial, and educational foundations. At bottom, their purpose was to upgrade the quality of life for Mexican-American and other Hispanic peoples, and in so doing for all of American society.

In its essence this was the struggle of a people in pursuit of the American dream. In quest of this dream, the GI Forum emerged as a guiding light by which its members and the broader society were visibly moved. Firm in its dedication to fundamental American ideals, the Forum set out to boldly challenge and transform, in an unprecedented way, the very structures and institutions of American society, institutions built upon double standards which rendered Mexican Americans lesser beneficiaries of the American dream. Given the magnitude of its charge, the Forum's growth and expansion drew on multiple undertakings. These included local self-help educational drives; state and national initiatives to ensure greater Mexican-American political representation; complex legal battles to desegregate school and jury systems in various southwestern states; programs to train, protect, and employ unskilled Mexican-American workers; and direct citizen challenges to businesses and corporations to promote greater accountability to the nation's Hispanic community. During the Forum's early years, these were highly innovative and frequently unprecedented involvements. The GI Forum, however, consistently implemented these strategies with positive and far-reaching impacts. That its membership succeeded in so many areas and in such lasting ways, with so few supporting material resources, marks the Forum's principal distinction. The Forum's successes were an inspiration to its people everywhere, and through the inspiration the organization instilled, it set the tone of postwar Mexican-American efforts to transcend second-class citizenship. Always the Forum was at the forefront, developing community strategies and innovations that eventually saw national applications by other groups during the 1960s and 1970s civil rights and Chicano movements.

This is the story of the American GI Forum from its inception in Texas in 1948 to recent years. By the very nature of the organization's accomplishments over the past five decades, the story here speaks particularly to Americans of Mexican descent. Yet the story that follows offers lessons and reinforcement for all Americans committed to social justice, and all people who believe in the possibility of racial equality. In its essence, the Forum's story is an inspiring American tale and a moving account of the human spirit.

Chapter 1

Veterans and Americans

The physical and emotional taxation of World War II was no less extreme for Mexican-American soldiers than for any other U. S. soldiers who saw combat. In many instances, the sacrifices of Mexican-American servicemen were particularly great. Raúl Morín's historic work *Among the Valiant*[1] documents the many contributions of these soldiers to American military victory during the war. For example, José P. Martínez of Colorado distinguished himself in battle against Japanese forces in the Pacific Theater at Attu in the Aleutian islands. On May 27, 1943, Martínez twice led his pinned-down platoon through heavy enemy rifle and machine-gun fire to capture a pass overlooking a key harbor. Martínez, awarded the Congressional Medal of Honor posthumously for his actions, became the first draftee in the Pacific to earn that distinction.[2] In Europe, Staff Sergeant Luciano Adams of Texas also earned a Congressional Medal of Honor for his heroic combat efforts. On October 28, 1944, Adams single-handedly eliminated three German machine-gun posts while taking heavy direct fire in the Montagne Forest of France.[3]

According to historian Albert Camarillo, Mexican-American soldiers distinguished themselves in nearly every major campaign of World War II:

> The heroes of Mexican descent were numerous, their bravery exemplified by their being the most decorated ethnic group of World War II. Many of the medals of valor granted to Chicanos were award-

ed posthumously. There was a disproportionate number of Mexican-American casualties relative to the group's percentage of the total population. Though Mexicans of Los Angeles, for example, accounted for approximately ten percent of the city's total population, they accounted for about twenty percent of the Angelenos killed in action. Losses were especially high in such "all Chicano companies" as Company E of the 141st Regiment of the 36th (Texas) division where all but twenty-three of the soldiers were killed in the Mediterranean campaigns.[4]

For the most part, these were not officers. These were infantrymen and gunboat attendants for whom front-line duty was the rule rather than the exception. Despite this, not a single Spanish-surnamed soldier was reported to have deserted, nor was an American of Mexican descent ever charged with cowardice or treason.[5] These were highly courageous individuals who fought with fervor and conviction for the nation they represented. The part they played in securing Allied victories overseas was an important one, and few of them lacked an understanding of this upon returning home at the war's end. Like other Americans, their sense of personal and collective accomplishment was immense.

Still, these servicemen returned to a society that had historically denied Mexican-Americans and others the full benefits of citizenship to which they were rightfully entitled, and they quickly found that the war had done little to change this. Throughout the southwestern United States, where Americans of Mexican descent had traditionally been relegated to second-class citizenship, discrimination and prejudice persisted. Despite their demonstrated courage and valor in defending their nation in war, Mexican-American veterans were no less subjected to continuing abuse of this sort. Aside from informal manifestations of prejudice and discrimination—racial threats and slurs, public signs, and social restrictions—returning Mexican-American servicemen came to experience more directly than ever before the discriminatory injustice and neglect of American institutions. Supposedly equal beneficiaries of the entitlements attendant to the GI Bill, these returning servicemen frequently found themselves denied the generally prompt and adequate receipt of the bill's financial, educational, and health benefits afforded their Anglo counterparts.

In Texas, the needs of Mexican-American veterans were perhaps greater than in any other state, yet official neglect of their circumstances and rights was distinctly pronounced. Compensation checks processed through the Veterans Administration were typically received six to eight months overdue and disability payments owed were often mistakenly reduced or totally eliminated without due process of review.[6] Furthermore, applications for formal schooling under the GI Bill were not being processed in time to allow Mexican-American veterans of the state to attend school, as had been intended.[7] Such delays presented real hardships for these veterans and their families, who experienced during these years especially significant need of medical care, social service attention, and educational and employment assistance.

The health care needs of returning Mexican-American servicemen were particularly great. Many had sustained severe casualties on the front lines of combat. Moreover, in their absence during the war years, their families had continued to experience among the nation's highest incidences of illness and disease due to poverty and discrimination, which had traditionally depressed their living conditions. According to one federal survey conducted in south Texas during the 1930s, for example, Mexican-Americans typically lived in one- or two-room frame shacks with dirt floors and outdoor toilets.[8] Reporting their findings, the survey investigators observed that many of the dwellings they studied were patched together from scraps of lumber, old signboards, tar paper, and flattened oil cans. Children slept on dirt floors, rolled up in quilts. Clothing was kept in boxes under beds or cupboards. Given these living conditions, the survey investigators concluded, it could not be surprising that sickness and disease were common in the *barrios*, notwithstanding the great efforts by Mexican families to ensure cleanliness and hygiene.

Corpus Christi, Nueces County, an area predominantly inhabited by Spanish-speaking families, especially reflected the Mexican-American population's need for improved health care. In 1948, fully 34 percent of the area's family dwelling units were classified as substandard by the city-county health unit. The death rate from tuberculosis was nearly twice the statewide average. Dysentery cases were the cause of nearly eight times as many deaths as in other parts of the state. And pneumonia-related deaths were over 20 percent higher than the state average.[9]

Despite these circumstances, GI Bill health and medical benefits were frequently denied or delayed to Mexican-Americans.[10] When such benefits were afforded to Mexican-American veterans, moreover, it was general practice to treat them (and their families) in segregated hospital wards.[11]

Unlike their Anglo counterparts, Mexican-American veterans of this era were not generally drawn to seek assistance from local American Legions or Veterans of Foreign Wars centers. These associations, which ostensibly welcomed and represented all veterans, were all-white organizations lacking at the time real awareness of or concern for Mexican Americans. Often Mexican Americans who did opt for mainstream participation were quickly made aware of prevalent cultural and ethnic prejudices. Lacking, then, a sense of confidence in traditional veterans organizations, Mexican-American veterans increasingly found themselves fighting in isolation for their rightful benefits and place within American society, and rarely were they successful.

During early 1948, a group of Mexican-American veterans in Corpus Christi decided to call a meeting to seek redress of the many hardships they were experiencing due to persistent discrimination and institutional neglect. Behind this effort was a 34-year-old physician named Hector P. García. A veteran who had attained the rank of major in the Army Medical Corps for his performance in Europe from 1942 to 1945, García knew firsthand what Mexican Americans had experienced and achieved overseas in combat. Moreover, as a respected physician and leader in the local Mexican-American community, García could speak with authority about the many needs of veterans and their families. Most of his patients were *mexicanos*,[12] and many were veterans. All seemed to share the same misfortunes for no other reason than that they were Mexican Americans.

More than seven hundred men attended the Corpus Christi gathering at the Lamar School Auditorium on March 26, 1948. The meeting forged a quick consensus among participants on the need to lobby for an improvement of their situation. To this end, they voted to form a permanent body and elected Hector García to lead it.

With purpose and pride, the group adopted the name of the American GI Forum, and in the name the organization's makeup and philosophy were projected. The absence of direct ethnic identification with the Mexican-American community was intentional and largely the result of García's thinking. The intent was to emphasize that members, though distinct in ethnic and cultural orientation, were just as American as Anglos. That they had served their nation honorably in the military on the front lines of combat accounted for the use of *GI* in the organizational title. *GI* had emerged during the war as a slang reference to the common soldier, whose clothing and equipment was government-issue. Finally, the term *Forum* was chosen to connote the group's commitment to open public discourse and to the principles and ideals of democracy.[13]

Soon a logo and an official constitution were developed, and in keeping with the Forum's name, they too highlighted the organization's fundamentally patriotic character. The logo showed the American flag complete with its red, white, and blue coloring, and thirteen stars representing the original American colonies. The thirteenth star appeared in the upper middle area of the design, above the organizational name. Symbolizing the biblical star of David, this star conveyed the organization's religious conscience.

The GI Forum constitution was drafted with considerable input from Hector García, but was the brainchild of a young Texas attorney by the name of Gustavo (Gus) García.[14] Though García patterned the Forum constitution after those of other veterans and community organizations, he marked its structure with unique qualities. A formal tenet of the group's objectives, for example, was to "secure the blessings of American democracy" through strictly non-violent means.[15] This institutional commitment to non-violence—a concept earlier developed by Mohandas Gandhi in India and later popularized in the United States by Dr. Martin Luther King, Jr.—was still somewhat ahead of its time in 1948 America.

The Forum's basic aims and objectives[16] were to:

- Aid needy and disabled veterans;
- Develop leadership by creating interest in the Spanish-speaking population to participate intelligently and wholeheartedly in community, civic, and political affairs;

- Advance understanding between citizens of various national origins and religious beliefs to develop a more enlightened citizenry and a greater America;
- Preserve and advance the basic principles of democracy, the religious and political freedoms of the individual, and equal social and economic opportunities for all citizens;
- Secure and protect for all veterans and their families, regardless of race, color, or creed, the privileges vested in them by the Constitution and laws of our country;
- Combat juvenile delinquency through a Junior GI Forum program which teaches respect for law and order, discipline, good sportsmanship, and the value of team work;
- Uphold and maintain loyalty to the Constitution and flag of the United States;
- Award scholarships to deserving students;
- Preserve and defend the United States of America from all enemies.

The Forum's founding principles suggest that, while formed as a local body, the organization had a national outlook from the outset. But national stature did not come to it easily or immediately. Instead, the Forum evolved in its first years into a viable state organization whose hard-fought battles proved largely successful as a result of the group's then unique and progressive local makeup.

More than any other factor in supporting the Forum's early growth and success was the inclusion of entire families in its framework. From its beginnings the Forum was as much a family organization as a veterans organization, with the participation of women and youths secured by constitutional decree. Structurally, women and young people, the wives and children of founding members, were incorporated as auxiliary members of the Forum with broad control over their own units—the "Ladies Auxiliary" and the "Junior GI Forum." In organizational meetings of the whole, however, women and junior members were afforded full voting power equal to that of senior, male members. In its time and place this constituted a most progressive format, although its foundations were basically conservative. To Mexican Americans, the family structure was a traditional source of strength and pride. Given the organization's efforts to claim Mexican Americans' rightful place in society, it should therefore come as little surprise that the family unit played a central role in the Forum's development.

The GI Forum's female members were particularly effective organizational leaders and fundraisers, despite the superficially social character of their activities (picnics, sales of tamales, and junior queen contests, among other undertakings).[17] Funds and donations derived from these activities, however small they may have appeared by most standards, were critical to support the organization's basic needs, from printing informational materials to defraying membership fees. (For this reason, an annual dues fee of only 25 cents was required of members in the Forum's early years.) The women of the organization were its moral backbone; their involvement and activities made the men's goals both more accessible and more meaningful. Moreover, time would prove these women to be effective leaders of broader community causes, in great measure thanks to their experiences as Forumeers.[18]

Youth members of the GI Forum were also valuable contributors to the organization's cause and development, first as enthusiastic agents of the Forum's expansion, and later as local, state, and national leaders, both within the organization and in other realms.[19] With the full involvement of each veteran's family, the organization was empowered to undertake vigorous efforts to ensure benefits and public assistance for its members with demonstrated support from the greater Mexican-American community. It was precisely this broad base of community support that Hector García drew upon to challenge the continuing neglect of Mexican-American veterans and their families in south Texas.

Under Dr. García's leadership, the Forum pressured leading officials of the Veterans Administration and local politicians in and around Corpus Christi to expedite pension payments and education vouchers, and to provide more equitable and timely medical treatment, for needy Mexican-American veterans. Furthermore, the doctor challenged the competence of the VA's adjudication board in San Antonio to determine fairly and accurately the pension qualifications of many Forum members; in support of his claim he presented numerous documented cases.[20]

Initially, local VA officials, following established policy, insisted that standing to present evidence of hardship was vested exclusively in individual veterans, not sponsoring organizations such as the

Forum. But because the Forum was able to present formidable documentation of member rights and needs in an indisputable and efficient manner, corrections in VA policy and practice were slowly but surely obtained. While some benefit delays had continued for as long as two years, within six weeks of the Forum's intervention most of its members began receiving payments and educational assistance.[21]

These gains prompted the Forum's growth as Mexican-American families in other areas began to hear of and gain interest in the Corpus Christi group's successes. By July of 1948, GI Forum groups had been formed in eleven towns surrounding Corpus Christi. By December of the same year, forty Texas communities had an American GI Forum chapter.[22]

For all these groups the initial undertakings were much the same as those of the Corpus Christi group. Benefit payments and enhanced medical attention generally carried top priority. Beyond this, the organization's pressure on local schools and colleges was highly successful in increasing educational and vocational training opportunities for Forum members, and in some cases in developing new programs for these purposes where none existed previously.[23]

Once established as an effective and growing veterans' organization, the Forum's scope of activities and concerns began to grow. Clearly underlying the inefficiencies and inequities encountered by Forum members were the more fundamental issues of prejudice and discrimination. Hector García and other emergent leaders of the Forum understood the organization's need to play an active role in combating these deeper problems if it was ever to enhance the quality of life for Mexican-American veterans and their families. Consequently, numerous committees and study groups were established by the Forum's founding chapter to deal specifically with potential involvements and undertakings in community housing, public education, voter participation, health care, and employment.[24] Along with the League of United Latin American Citizens (LULAC), the leading Latino civil rights organization of the day, the Forum began sponsoring "back-to-school" and "pay your poll tax" drives in various Texas towns.[25] Beyond this, the organization began to formally challenge discriminatory policies and practices of various local and state institutions, including the Texas Selective Service Board (where the Hispanic population—20 percent of the state—was without a single representative on any county draft board); city and county hospitals (which practiced ward segregation); and the post office (which hired Mexican Americans in delivery positions but prohibited them from working behind service windows).[26]

In all these areas the Forum experienced opposition, but in most instances the group's involvement brought improvements. More often than not these improvements were less than entirely satisfactory, but in the times and places of their occurrence they constituted unprecedented victories. Always the Forum's aims and emphasis rested with promoting equal access and participation for Mexican Americans in the various sectors and institutions comprising American life. With every undertaking, the Forum and the Mexican-American people took a step toward those ends. This movement forward encouraged Dr. García and his organization to push ahead in seeking to defend the rights of Mexican Americans in an increasingly larger arena. Nothing confirmed and motivated the organization's work more than the Felix Longoria controversy of early 1949.

In the second week of that year, Hector García received a request for his assistance in facilitating the proper burial of Private Felix Longoria, a Mexican-American soldier whose remains had just been returned home from overseas nearly four years after his death in combat in the Philippines. Sara Moreno, an acquaintance of the doctor through her involvement in a GI Forum-sponsored girls club, sought García's assistance on behalf of her sister, Beatriz Longoria, the soldier's widow.

Earlier in the week Mrs. Longoria had been informed by Tom Kennedy, the new owner of the Rice Funeral Home in Longoria's home town of Three Rivers, Texas, that he would arrange for the soldier's burial. Unfortunately, in making funeral arrangements, Kennedy invoked two biting reminders of the Mexican-American community's second-class status, neither of which sat well with Longoria's widow. First, Kennedy informed the family that the burial would be in the town's segregated "Mexican cemetery." Second, he denied the family's request for use of the funeral home's chapel to hold a wake in honor of Private Longoria on grounds that local "whites would not like it."[27]

When García learned of this, he immediately contacted Kennedy by telephone in Three Rivers and appealed to him on behalf of the Longoria family to handle the burial and wake as requested by Mrs. Longoria. Kennedy held firm, however, that the chapel would not be made available. Historian Carl Allsup cites the exchange as follows:

GARCÍA: But why, Mr. Kennedy?

KENNEDY: Well, you see, it's this way. This is a small town, and you know how it is. I'm sure you understand. I am the only funeral home here, and I just have to do what the white people want. The white people just won't like it.

GARCÍA: But, Mr. Kennedy, this man is a veteran, a soldier who was killed in action and he is worthy of our greatest honors. Doesn't that make a difference?

KENNEDY: No, that doesn't make a difference. You know how the Latin people get drunk and lay around all the time. The last time the Latin Americans used the home they had fights and got drunk and raised lots of noise, and it didn't look so good. We have not let them use it [the chapel] and we don't intend to let them start now. I don't dislike Mexican people, but I have to run my business . . . you understand, the whites here won't like it.[28]

García knew his organization could not stand by idly on a matter of such blatant disregard for the rights and integrity of Mexican-American veterans and community members. After his conversation with Kennedy, García telephoned George Groh, a local reporter for the *Corpus Christi Caller-Times*, who had been covering the Forum's activities from its inception. García explained the situation and repeated his conversation with Kennedy. He also informed Groh that the Forum's founding chapter would hold a protest meeting the following evening. Groh in turn contacted Kennedy for verification of

García's account. The funeral director confirmed the doctor's claim that use of the chapel had been denied. When Groh asked if refusal had been based on Longoria's ethnic background, Kennedy replied, "We never have made a practice of letting Mexicans use the chapel and we don't want to start now."[29]

After contacting Groh, Dr. García telegrammed letters of protest to various members of the state legislature and of the Texas congressional delegation in Washington, D. C. Among those receiving a telegram was newly elected U. S. Senator Lyndon B. Johnson. García had never met Johnson, but he was strongly encouraged to write the young senator by Congressman John Lyle, a mutual friend. In his telegram to Johnson, García described the Longoria situation as "a direct contradiction of those same principles for which this American soldier made the supreme sacrifice in giving his life for his country, and for the same people who now deny him the last funeral rites deserving of any American hero, regardless of his origin."[30]

The following day, Groh called Kennedy to reconfirm his position before going to print. Kennedy altered his language somewhat, indicating that he would "discourage" the chapel's use, though not refuse other services for the Longoria burial. But Kennedy neither denied nor retracted his comments of the previous day and Groh proceeded with his article accordingly.[31]

At this point events assumed proportions that neither Dr. García nor the Longoria family could have envisioned. Responding to the *Caller-Times'* involvement in the case, the mayor of Three Rivers, J. K. Montgomery, sent an urgent telegram to the American GI Forum's headquarters. According to Montgomery, who had just interviewed Kennedy, the whole controversy was "a mistake." Kennedy had not refused use of his facilities and was not refusing them, said Montgomery. Arrangements could still be made, he added, to use the funeral home, if desired by the Longoria family, or the local American Legion hall could arrange the burial with full military honors. The mayor even offered his own home for the services, if necessary.

Notwithstanding Montgomery's seemingly conciliatory effort to clarify and resolve the conflict, García and other Forum leaders remained apprehensive about letting the matter drop. According to

Longoria family members, Mayor Montgomery's account of Kennedy's position in the controversy simply did not correspond to their experiences with him.

Later in the morning, telegrams received by García from U. S. Representatives John Lyle and Lloyd M. Bentsen, Jr., condemned Kennedy's actions. Both congressmen promised to cooperate with the state's Good Neighbor Commission to seek an appropriate resolution in the matter. (The Good Neighbor Commission, created to enhance relations between Mexico and the United States, as well as among Texas citizens, did ultimately become involved in the Longoria affair and generally sided with the GI Forum in the matter. However, due to the commission's sensitivity to public opinion on all sides of the controversy, and its consequent hesitance to endorse unequivocally the Forum's position, its involvement in the case was not fully to the Forum's satisfaction.) State Senator Rogers Kelley deplored the Rice Funeral Home's "un-American and reprehensible conduct,"[32] and Governor Beauford Jester obtained a personal commitment from Kennedy to proceed with Longoria's funeral as requested by the family.[33] Even nationally syndicated columnist Walter Winchell noted the events in Three Rivers, commenting: "The state of Texas, which looms so large on the map, looks mighty small tonight . . ."[34]

That evening Hector García proceeded with the Forum's planned protest meeting, which was attended by nearly one thousand people. The gathering was peaceful but highly charged, especially in light of growing national attention. As possible avenues of response to the situation were discussed, García interrupted the meeting to share a telegram he had just received:

> I deeply regret to learn that the prejudice of some individuals extends beyond this life. I have no authority over civilian funeral homes. Nor does the federal government. However, I have today made arrangements to have Felix Longoria buried with full military honors in Arlington National Cemetery here at Washington where the honored dead of our nation's wars rest. Or, if his family prefers to have his body interred nearer his home, he can be re-buried at Fort Sam Houston National Military Cemetery at San Antonio. There will be no cost. If his widow desires to have reburial in either cemetery she should send me a collect telegram before his body is unloaded from an army transport at San Francisco, January 13. This injustice and prejudice is deplorable. I am happy to have a part in seeing that

this Texas hero is laid to rest with the honor and dignity his service deserves.

Lyndon B. Johnson, USS[35]

Highly moved by Senator Johnson's action, the meeting's partic-ipants voted in favor of contributing funds to the Longoria family to assist them in traveling to Washington, D.C. for the suggested burial at Arlington National Cemetery. About nine hundred dollars was col-lected at the meeting, and the campaign to secure needed additional funds proceeded thereafter. But the Longoria matter did not end there, nor did the GI Forum's involvement in the case as the Mexican-American community's central representative.

Put on the defensive by the support García had secured from Lyndon Johnson and other influential persons, the Anglo leadership of Three Rivers engaged in a concerted effort to suggest that the Longoria affair had been falsely portrayed by GI Forum leaders and media outside of the area. The local chamber of commerce endorsed a statement issued by Tom Kennedy in which he denied that he had ever refused Beatriz Longoria use of his funeral home's chapel, asserting that he had discouraged its use because he believed Mrs. Longoria's wishes had differed from those of the deceased soldier's parents. The suggestion here was that the problem arose as a result of conflicts not between Anglos and Mexican Americans, but rather between Mexican Americans themselves. Stories were circulated around Three Rivers that Guadalupe Longoria, the dead soldier's father, disapproved of the Forum's involvement in the matter, dis-liked Hector García, and was insulted by the collections taken up to support his son's burial in Washington.[36]

On January 20 the local newspaper, *Three Rivers News*, ran an editorial wholeheartedly defending the town's goodwill and con-demning Lyndon Johnson for "hasty" involvement in the Longoria incident. According to the paper, "No town in south Texas [had] bet-ter relations with Americans of Mexican descent . . ." and Johnson's proposal to bury the deceased Longoria at Arlington National Cemetery was unnecessary because the people of Three Rivers "were prepared to bury their deceased brother and had even arranged the fir-ing squad [for a twenty-one gun salute]." The editorial concluded that

Tom Kennedy had acted improperly but only out of sincere concern for Longoria's widow, whom he believed to be disliked by the Longoria family. In short, Kennedy had been misquoted and misjudged.[37]

Shortly after the editorial appeared, the American Legion of San Antonio passed a resolution berating the "careless and immature actions of people in high and honorable places [which brought] harmful humiliation and embarrassment . . . to the Kennedy family . . . the good people of Three Rivers and the state of Texas." According to the resolution, the people of Three Rivers had enjoyed "at all times peaceful, orderly and most pleasant relations among the races."[38]

Grandstanding of this kind, coupled with the broad public resentment that it inspired, encouraged Longoria family members to accept Lyndon Johnson's invitation to bury their hero at Arlington Cemetery in Washington. But even with Longoria's burial there with honors on February 16, 1949, the controversy in Three Rivers was not laid to rest. The day following the funeral, Texas State Representative J. F. Gray called for an investigation of the incidents leading to the Longoria controversy, and a special committee was authorized for this purpose.[39]

Ostensibly created to determine the true story of what initially transpired between Tom Kennedy and the Longoria family, Gray's committee would be more accurately described as in an effort to discredit claims that racial discrimination against Mexican Americans had created the controversy. Already Gray had unsuccessfully proposed a bill to eliminate the Texas Good Neighbor Commission on grounds that its involvement in matters such as the Longoria affair constituted unnecessary and undesirable state intervention.

Despite the all-white composition of the state's five-member special investigative committee, Hector García welcomed its formation and called for its hearings to be open to the public. Tom Sutherland, chairman of the Good Neighbor Commission, offered to resign if the committee investigation found duplicity in the commission's involvement in the case. The committee hearings were held during the first week of April, 1949, in the Chamber of Commerce Building at Three Rivers. The Bee County sheriff (a man noted for his condescension toward Mexican Americans) oversaw the proceedings with loaded pistols. Given the location and tenor of the hearings, few Mexican Americans attended.

From the outset, the state special committee made clear that permissible evidence would be severely restricted. Only testimony directly related to the funeral home incident was allowed, and general remarks or testimony concerning prejudice or discrimination in Texas were deemed inadmissible. Throughout the hearings Kennedy and Three Rivers representatives denounced the American GI Forum, the Good Neighbor Commission, and Lyndon Johnson as troublemakers and political opportunists. Letters and statements by Tom Kennedy to Beatriz Longoria and Hector García clarifying that he had never denied Longoria use of his chapel (but only discouraged it), as well as Mayor J. K. Montgomery's January 11 telegram to García, were presented as proof of the goodwill that had been demonstrated to Mexican Americans by Three Rivers Anglos.[40]

But Hector García and GI Forum attorney Gus García presented convincing evidence to counter such claims. Tom Sutherland of the Good Neighbor Commission testified, for example, that Kennedy had confided in him that he simply could not allow "Mexicans" to use his chapel.[41] Notarized statements from Sara Moreno, Beatriz Longoria, George Groh, and others similarly suggested that racial bias played a significant part in preventing Kennedy from honoring stated family wishes for Felix Longoria's burial.[42]

Groh's testimony was particularly revealing. The reporter confirmed that Kennedy had clearly stated to him local "whites would object" to his granting the Longoria's use of the Three Rivers Funeral Home's chapel, despite Kennedy's being reminded that his comments were for the record. Furthermore, Groh testified, Kennedy had made the comment, also for the record, that he did not want to make a practice of letting Mexican Americans use the chapel.[43]

A dramatic final statement from Private Longoria's father, Guadalupe Longoria, fully repudiated claims that he disapproved of Beatriz, his daughter-in-law, of her handling of the funeral plans, or of the GI Forum's involvement after the exchange with Kennedy. On the contrary, Longoria testified, he had requested the Forum's assistance, notwithstanding attempts by the president of the Three Rivers Chamber of Commerce, the mayor, and the city secretary to persuade him that Forum involvement in the matter was unnecessary and undesirable.[44] The father's testimony concluded:

> I want it clearly understood that I am very grateful to Dr. García and the American GI Forum for their efforts on our behalf . . . to other organizations . . . and particularly to Senator Johnson. If any embarrassment has been caused by this case to anyone, I am sorry, but after all, I did not create a feeling of prejudice which seems to exist in many places in Texas against people of my national origin. Other people are responsible for that. I think we would only be fooling ourselves to try to leave the impression that people of Mexican descent are treated the same as anyone else throughout the state of Texas.[45]

Notwithstanding persuasive notarized statements indicating Kennedy's racial bias, concurring testimony, and clear evidence of locally segregated "Mexican" and "white" cemeteries and burial practices, the state's special investigative committee released a majority report on April 7, 1949, concluding "There was no discrimination on the part of the undertaker of Three Rivers relative to the proposed burial of . . . the deceased Felix Longoria."[46] The committee concluded that Mr. Kennedy had acted in the belief that "strained relations" existed in the Longoria family, and that in denying the family's equal use of his facilities he had only been concerned for the widow's best interests. Four of the five committee members signed the report. Anglo leaders of Three Rivers invoked the majority report as "proof" of the town's sense of justice and fair play. Many observers, however, criticized the obvious slant of evidence incorporated into the majority statement. State Senator Rogers Kelley called it "a tragic blot on the democracy of Texas and the United States."[47]

Frank Oltorf, the committee's lone dissenting member, submitted a minority report stating that he could not concur in the majority report without violating his sense of justice and intellectual honesty.[48] Oltorf concluded that indisputable evidence from the hearings had clearly established discrimination was involved in the incident. "I cannot look into the heart of Mr. Kennedy," Oltorf wrote, "to ascertain his true intent but can only accept his oral words, which appear to me discriminatory." Shortly after Oltorf's minority report was released, one of the majority report's co-signers, Byron Tinsley, asked that his name be withdrawn. Citing hasty action and new evidence, Tinsley requested additional investigation, indicating that without this he would be forced to submit his own report.[49]

Although Tinsley's motivation for the change remain unclear, his action, coupled with Frank Oltorf's initial repudiation of the committee's findings, underscored the majority report's incredibility. In the end, the document was never incorporated into the state legislative record and the matter was effectively dropped. Thus, against near overwhelming odds, Hector García and the GI Forum effectively prevailed in the Longoria controversy at Three Rivers.

Beyond its significance as a widely recognized victory for the upstart GI Forum, the Longoria affair served notice that unchallenged prejudice and discrimination against Mexican Americans in Texas and other states was a phenomenon of the past. Mexican Americans had sacrificed with distinction their blood, sweat, tears and toil for their country in overseas combat against totalitarianism and Nazi and Japanese notions of racial superiority. In doing so they had proven their faith in and commitment to the American dream, and so had earned the right to pursue that dream in their own lives back home. The GI Forum's successful challenge to the Three Rivers establishment highlighted the possibility that Mexican Americans could realize the American dream through grassroots organization and community activism. In pursuit of that possibility, Mexican Americans everywhere turned increasingly to the Forum and to a generation of inspiring social change.

Chapter 2

Building From the Ground Up

Young or old, anyone associated with the Forum in its formative years can recount stories of traveling with family and friends to far-away places on weekends or vacations, to meet with other member families or potential members. Wherever these early Forumeers traveled they spread the word about their organization. After the Longoria incident, community interest surrounding the Forum grew substantially. Calls and inquiries from Texas and elsewhere about initiating new Forum chapters came increasingly to Hector García and other first-generation organizational leaders.

"There was no master plan, no blueprint for the Forum's expansion," García would say in a November 1981 interview–only a continued need to address the issues and problems confronting Mexican Americans throughout American society. However great and unprecedented the organization's initial victories may have been in Corpus Christi and Texas, beyond those successes persisted the same disabling experiences for millions of Mexican Americans in other cities and states. Mexican-American veterans had little or no wherewithal to combat denials or delays of their pension payments or benefits, of their access to decent medical care and hospital treatment, or of their employment rights and opportunities. Furthermore, they had insufficient recourse to the prejudice and discrimination that denied most Mexican Americans adequate education, decent housing, and just treatment under the law. It was with those who most felt the weight of these conditions that the GI Forum found its need and acceptance to be greatest. These were working- and lower working-class Mexican Americans, and regional distinctions notwithstanding, the Forum's appeal to them was particularly powerful and well-timed.

Coupled with compelling community needs was an expanding awareness that most historians attribute directly to experiences gleaned during World War II. During the war years, Mexican-American men and women were exposed to new possibilities in areas ranging from military-related service and travel to non-traditional employment. This exposure inspired a new sense of possibilities. According to Raúl Morín, new thoughts and dreams entered the Mexican-American consciousness:

> In the old days, our lives were governed mostly by patterns set by our elders. We had accepted without question edicts, taboos, restrictions, traditions, and customs that our ancestors had brought over from the old country. Many such were long since outdated in Mexico proper. After having been to many other parts of the world, meeting other people from different parts of the country, we cast aside these old beliefs and we began anew in America.

The changes brought about by the war were as profound for Mexican-American women as for their male counterparts. According to Albert Camarillo,

> Though Chicanas in large numbers had long worked outside the home, they now moved in unprecedented numbers into individual, manufacturing, and office jobs. As the manpower shortage developed, Chicanas, like American women everywhere, filled the labor gaps. War-related employment as factory workers and other non traditional jobs, especially clerical positions, became available to many Mexican women. This opportunity to work outside the home offered them a sense of independence and importance.

These more individually driven inducements to change inspired attention as well to revised social aspirations among the Mexican-American World War II generation, who came increasingly to see continuing second-class citizenship as unacceptable. This created in turn a new sense of purpose and responsibility. Díaz de Cossío, *et al.* describe the phenomenon:

> It was participation in the second world war that gave Mexicans a new perspective. It made them conscious that as citizens of the U. S. who had proved their loyalty and valor in the defense of American principles, they could and should fight to exercise all of their rights to nationality and citizenship which until now had been denied.[1]

This expanding community consciousness resulted in the rapid emergence after the war of various new civic organizations targeted to Mexican-American constituencies. Most of these groups, many led by veterans, were local or regional, such as the Community Services Organization (CSO)[2] and the Latin American Veterans Association[3] in California, for example. The GI Forum quickly became the most significant of these new groups throughout much of the southwestern and midwestern United States.

In addition to unique historical circumstances, novel organizing strategies and dynamic leadership account for the Forum's early successes. Invariably, Forum organizers would travel to town after town and state after state, stressing a compelling combination of essentially conservative and yet progressive values: patriotism, family, religious faith, educational equity, and non-violence. But the pivotal element the Forum brought was a way for Mexican Americans to organize their values around a new appreciation and enthusiasm for democratic process, civic participation, and community building.

Early Forum leaders had learned from experience that funds could never be a primary source of organizational success, due to the limited financial resources of Mexican-American people; but so long as the organization remained true to its objectives, its members would be supportive. The truly significant factor marking the difference between long-term Forum achievements or failure, then, would be each chapter's ability to make strategic use of its financial and human capital. This required sound organization and leadership.[4]

Thus, wherever new chapters were established, their members were roundly prepared with community organizing and leadership skills. The defined structure and format of the Forum's founding chapter were uniformly applied to expansion chapters: Officers were elected, constitutions and bylaws were drafted, committees and task forces were assigned, and meeting dates and chapter agendas were set.

Meetings were run by *Robert's Rules of Order*. What evolved was a democratic system on a small scale.

Hector García and other organizational leaders gave each new chapter its initial breath of life, but thereafter local leadership and volition within the larger organizational scheme was encouraged. Local leadership was determined by the local membership, as were the central focal points of each chapter's involvement. Internal organizational decisions evolved through careful discussion and debate. The result was the development of a wide set of locally developed skills and insights that enhanced the Forum's internal strength, as well as its capacity to wield influence within the broader American political context.[5]

The Forum's initial growth and expansion was largely the product of input from several younger and highly capable men who surrounded Hector García: Gus García, the attorney who had masterminded the Forum's governance structure and its legal strategy during the Longoria hearings; James De Anda, also an attorney, who like Gus García would later gain national prominence in several landmark desegregation suits; Ed Idar, Jr., a journalist and protégé of the noted educator Dr. George I. Sánchez at the University of Texas at Austin; Vicente Ximenes, a graduate student of economics at the University of New Mexico; and Cris Alderete, founder of the Alba Club at the University of Texas, an attorney, and later city commissioner of Del Rio, Texas. The vision and vigor of these young men set the tone for the organization's development beyond Corpus Christi. Idar, elected GI Forum state (Texas) chairman in 1951, was instrumental in initiating the organization's first monthly news bulletin (later called *The Forumeer*), an important mechanism for organizational communication and expansion. Along with Gus García and James De Anda, Cris Alderete played a major role in legally challenging school and jury segregation in various Texas districts. Their successes in these areas remain important and informative antecedents of contemporary Chicano civil rights battles.[6]

Idar and Alderete were particularly instrumental in organizing the Forum's expansion throughout Texas. With Dr. García in his Edsel, or alone in their own or borrowed cars, Idar and Alderete logged thousands of miles on countless weekends and holidays up and down the state, organizing chapters. In two weeks they would visit as many as twenty towns and cities. Such travel must have been extremely taxing, particularly for men operating on time taken from already exacting careers. That they undertook the burden, and did so with such vigor, speaks to their conviction in the Forum's aims and ideals.

Underscoring the organization's compelling objectives for young men such as Idar and Alderete was the inspiration of Hector García. His care in ensuring the Forum's long-term viability and direction cannot be overstated. From the earliest days of the organization's development, García responded to virtually every expression of interest in forming new chapters in the area surrounding Corpus Christi. On his own time and with his own money he would travel wherever necessary to assist needy Mexican-American veterans and their families in forming new GI Forum chapters. It was García who insisted on meaningful roles for women and youth in the Forum's evolving structure. It was García who best advocated greater local and state governmental attention to Mexican-American community rights and needs. It was García who most effectively sensitized Anglo leaders and citizens to the suffering and injustice that beset Mexican Americans in Texas.

García's leadership was informed by several key personal qualities, which amounted to significant strengths in the Forum's development: an appreciation of people; a total conviction as to the Forum's cause and justification; and a tacit understanding of his own limitations. According to Julie Leininger Pycior, for example:

> Proud, confident, with an air of serious commitment, Dr. García threw himself into seeing patients, calling organizers, receiving visitors. He focused intently on individuals, quickly learning each one's name, looking each in the eye. His frenetic, charismatic style was balanced by an ability to attract younger, more methodical people such as Cris Alderete and Ed Idar. Unlike LULACkers, they did not have to emphasize their knowledge of English and their professional status in order to prove their U.S. citizenship to skeptical Anglos. No matter how poor or dark-skinned, a veteran had the best possible U.S. pedigree. "We were Americans, not 'spics' or 'greasers'," García recalled, "because when you fight for your country in a World War, against an alien philosophy, faciscm, you are an American and proud to be in America." His American GI Forum proved to be an effective combination of Mexican community roots and U.S. identity; by the

end of 1948 the GI Forum had chapters throughout South Texas, except in [political] machine-dominated counties such as Duval.[7]

García's tactics were controversial. According to Ralph Guzmán, García stirred the public with

> shocking statistics of infant mortality, tuberculosis, discrimination in housing, restaurants, swimming pools, barber shops and other places of public accommodation. He identified city halls, and other institutions that would not hire Mexicans. Like Rosa Parks who precipitated the Birmingham, Alabama bus boycott, García [inspired] social movement . . .

The doctor's unbending commitment to his cause was difficult for even his most ardent mainstream critics to disregard. His ability to command respect through compassion and sincerity brought him influence and friendship during these years with Texas politicians no less influential than Lyndon Johnson, Lloyd Bentsen, Jr., John Connally, John Lyle, and Jim Wright. In addition, it earned him respect beyond the mainstream political arena.

One individual whose life and work García touched in a particularly special way was the author Edna Ferber, who contacted the doctor in early 1950 to gather information for a book she was writing about Texas. Ferber wanted to write a novel that would portray all aspects of life in Texas, including the state's Mexican-American people. She had heard of García's work with the Forum and requested to meet with him for a firsthand account of his experiences. For three weeks she visited García in Corpus Christi, walking with him daily through the streets of the city's *mexicano* community, and traveling with him and other Forumeers around south Texas. The result, *Giant,* eventually became a bestseller upon which Hollywood filmmakers later based a major motion picture.[8]

A distinguishing feature of Ferber's book is her effort to depict the plight of Mexican Americans in Texas. In several important scenes the book's protagonist, Leslie, a northern socialite, is introduced to the hard realities of Texas politics and society. In one scene, Leslie is appalled to learn that the gates of south Texas ranches are locked shut on election day, to prevent Mexican-American workers from voting in town. Later, she encounters the brutal and inhumane treatment to which "Mexicans" are subjected by border ranchers and law enforcement authorities. In an effort to explain, Leslie's local confidant, Uncle Bawley, admits at one point,

> Strictly speaking—which hardly anybody does—why, what with picking cotton and fruit and now the Valley is all planted with vegetables, a big new industry, and the old railroad building days and all, why you might say the whole of Texas was built on the backs. . . of Mexicans.

Ferber's work offered Americans one of the first popular portrayals of broad-based inequality in America beyond the circumstances confronting black Americans.

In organizing the GI Forum, then, García touched increasing numbers of persons outside of the Mexican-American community. Not surprisingly, though, his work and accomplishments endeared him mainly to his own people. To them García embodied and inspired courage, integrity, and resolve. These qualities would characterize García even as threats to his life and challenges to his work became commonplace. Phone calls from reactionary fringe elements to García's home or office promised violence against the doctor, break-ins into his medical offices, and vigilante "welcoming committees" in towns García visited. Some even targeted the doctor's family for threat and humiliation. Being the only Hispanic family in a white neighborhood increased García's vulnerability. Years later, the doctor's daughter, Cecilia Akers, would recall:

> I could not ride my bike in our neighborhood without being taunted by the white children. "Why don't you just go back to Mexico?!?" they would scream at me. Of course, we were Texans and our people had been there longer than the white families. We didn't know anything about Mexico; our country was the United States! . . . Often, the neighborhood kids would spit at us or put snakes in our mailbox. This treatment was hard to imagine coming from other children. I later came to understand that it was inspired by a blind hatred and ignorance that had nothing really to do with me as a person. It had to do with the system that promoted these things, and with my father's efforts to challenge it.[9]

The most serious threats never materialized, but few who lived during those years would deny that physical danger was always a possibility for the doctor wherever he traveled, and there were actual attempts to harm or intimidate García and other Forum leaders.

Beyond physical threats, García and other Forumeers confronted increasingly prevalent efforts outside of the *mexicano* community to paint the GI Forum as a communist-inspired or subversive organization. Invariably, suggestions of this nature were mainly directed at García, who was frequently labeled an "agitator," a "red," and a threat to American society. Underlying these attacks, however, was a thinly veiled agenda to deny equal rights and opportunities to Mexican-American people.

Despite the many challenges, García moved ahead aggressively. "Sure I knew I could be killed," the doctor would later admit, "and I wasn't so bold that it didn't bother me. But there was just so much to do, we couldn't stop. We just had to keep moving ahead." In this way, García marked the standard of dedication that Idar, Alderete, and others followed in building the Texas organization. Soon Vicente Ximenes, a young friend of García, would take inspiration from the doctor and his Texas colleagues and start organizing GI Forums in New Mexico and other states, initiating the organization's national expansion.

During World War II, Ximenes had served as a bombardier and earned the Distinguished Flying Cross for his combat performance in North Africa. After serving seven years as a major in the Army Air Corps, Ximenes left the service in 1949 to enroll in a master's degree program in economics at the University of New Mexico. He was well into his course of study at the university when in the summer of 1950 he briefly visited his friend Hector García in Corpus Christi. García conveyed to Ximenes the nature of his organization's struggle in Texas and the need to dramatically improve the circumstances of Mexican-American veterans and their families. Ximenes knew firsthand that the doctor's agenda was timely and important. Furthermore, he knew García well and perceived in him the dedication and demeanor of a man destined to help right historical and institutional wrongs. He knew of García's sincerity and responsibility, and was moved by the doctor's struggle to do something concrete to right these wrongs.

Ximenes returned to Albuquerque and immediately founded a GI Forum chapter there. Then with the help of Louis and Isabelle Téllez, a young married couple and charter members of the Albuquerque chapter, he boldly set out to broaden the Forum's scope and influence. On countless organizing trips around (and later outside of) the state, the young scholar would study in the back seat of the car as Louis Téllez or other accompanying Forumeers drove them from town to town.[10] Their efforts to build a following were not much different, and certainly no less exacting, than efforts to organize Texas had been. In place after place, Ximenes and Téllez emphasized the Forum's principle tenets—patriotism, family, religious faith, and education. They traveled on their own time and limited personal budgets. And wherever they traveled they found community enthusiasm for the organization. Only the names of the towns they visited and the roads they traveled were distinct from the Forum organizing experience in Texas.[11] By 1951, New Mexico officially became the second American GI Forum state organization, adopting in that year its first constitution, charter, and state officers. The Forum's development and influence in New Mexico was marked thereafter.

Through the rapid growth and success of the New Mexico organization, García and Ximenes were convinced of the viability of further organizational expansion to other states. Working together they began formulating modest goals for expansion. But with the growing call among Mexican Americans for a more just and equal place in American society, coupled with the return of thousands of new Mexican-American veterans from the Korean conflict, their initial expectations were far surpassed. By the mid-1950s, nearly ten states with sizable Mexican-American populations had requested assistance in organizing new Forum chapters. With García, Idar, Alderete, and other Texas leaders increasingly constrained by involvements in their home state, Vicente Ximenes assumed principal responsibility for responding to these requests; and so on his shoulders was placed the responsibility of leading the Forum's push towards national status. He picked up where he had left off in New Mexico and traveled to state after state, setting organizational processes in motion.

While Ximenes and other male leaders were the first engines of and contributors to the Forum's national growth and development, women were formidable and creative conspirators.[12] From its earliest days, the GI Forum, was heavily influenced by the mothers, sisters, girlfriends, wives, and daughters of the male Forumeers. Throughout the Forum's various stages of growth, they were incorporated wholeheartedly into the group's organizational framework. Initially, the women's focus was to support the work and concerns of the organization's male members. This was a function of both the era in which the Forum was established and the organization's emphasis on the priorities of its veteran base, which was overwhelmingly male. For the most part, this work entailed fundraising activities of a social character: *tamaladas*,[13] barbecues, dances, and later beauty contests. Due mainly to the Forum women's efforts, the larger organization was able to generate revenue that supported expanded activities and maintained minimal membership dues. This in turn attracted a wider membership and encouraged member enthusiasm and retention.

Support activities remained a central component of the GI Forum women's program for many years. Yet Forum women were increasingly called upon to take on challenging community leadership roles and activities as they became more involved in the organization. This was particularly the case as the Forum's activities expanded dramatically beyond veterans and local affairs into the larger national movement for minority civil rights. GI Forum efforts to affect U. S. civil rights policies eventually brought female members of the organization to the forefront of local, state, and national decision-making processes. Most of the Forum's women members came to this work without significant political experience. They responded well, however, to the challenges of civic leadership, proving to be effective community organizers and advocates.

Isabelle Téllez, one of the Forum's elder stateswomen, recalls the pivotal role GI Forum women played during the group's early years. According to Téllez, women played central roles in developing new GI Forum chapters and initiatives. For example, women were involved early on as leaders of Forum-sponsored voter registration drives and community service programs. Additionally, they were vocal and effective lobbyists for equal opportunity legislation in the states and localities where Forumeers were able to secure such measures on lawmakers' agendas.[14] In fact, GI Forum women leaders such as Molly Faid Galván of Colorado, Nellie Navarro of Kansas, Dominga Coronado and Margarita Simón of Texas, and Isabelle Téllez of New Mexico were motivating forces underlying the Forum's growth and success in their own and other Forum states.

Molly Galván originated the concept of a national Forum women's group, and shepherded its realization along with Isabelle Téllez, Nellie Navarro, and others at the first national GI Forum convention in 1956.[15] Galván, a tireless worker, proved an influential Forum leader in the organization's early days. She helped to establish a regional reporting and communications structure that greatly facilitated the Forum's expansion. She was also instrumental in organizing GI Forum chapters in Colorado, Utah, and other states.[16]

Like Galván, Nellie Navarro was the originator of bold undertakings aiding the Forum's development. Navarro, a Kansas resident, was largely responsible for that state's development as a GI Forum stronghold. A tiny woman only four feet, ten inches tall, Navarro embodied the determination of all Forumeers against the formidable adversities that confronted them. Navarro tackled the myriad civil rights issues of the day with an effectiveness and resolve few men or women could rival. In Dodge City, Navarro's home town, her efforts were so revered that a local park was eventually named in her honor.[17]

Dominga Coronado, a past national Forum officer and still an active Forum women's leader today, was a revered community activist from the outset. With her late husband, Gregorio, Coronado undertook extensive—and frequently dangerous—civil rights projects to desegregate restaurants, theaters, and schools around New Braunfels, Texas.

Margarita Símon of Texas developed and edited the Austin-based *El Demócrata*, a Forum-sponsored community newspaper that highlighted the organization's local activities and events, as well as key issues and challenges. Simón became increasingly active through her work with the Forum in leading city-wide initiatives to address local law enforcement and community health problems in Austin.[18]

Finally, Isabelle Téllez was a leading figure in the development of the GI Forum's New Mexico chapter. Her involvements ranged from leading voter registration and back-to-school drives to organizing local and state Forum conferences. In addition, from the 1960s through the mid-1980s, Téllez ably assisted her husband, Louis, who was appointed to establish and administer the Forum's national office in Albuquerque, New Mexico.[19] She substantially helped to advance Forum national governance processes, including the organization of national board meetings, conferences, and programs.

The most concentrated involvement of Forum women came in the area of education. Women leaders, many of them mothers and teachers, took on the issue of Mexican-American educational rights with special concern. These women had much to do with the decision to adopt the Forum's official motto: "Education Is Our Freedom, and Freedom Should Be Everybody's Business." They also played an important role in persuading the Forum's male leadership to make school desegregation a perennial focus of organizational activity during the 1950s.[20]

To complement these contributions to Mexican-American educational progress, Forum women developed innovative local scholarship programs, which the organization later institutionalized nationally.[21] Each year, monies raised by the activities and special events were allotted for scholarships to needy and deserving high school and college students who would otherwise be unable to continue their studies. Young people themselves were given great responsibility for fundraising and recipient selection. The very creation of such a scholarship program did much to encourage youth participation in the Forum, and thus reinforced the organization's family flavor. Aimed at expanding the educational opportunities of talented high school students, these efforts played an important part in developing a pipeline of future Mexican-American leaders and professionals, long before federal affirmative action and higher education scholarship programs were developed.

GI Forum women were forerunners in the development of adult and women's educational programs targeted at needy Hispanic Americans. As early as the mid-1950s, GI Forum women's groups sponsored and participated in grassroots leadership training conferences of their own design. These were revolutionary undertakings in their time, and highly effective mechanisms to develop the organizational and leadership capacities of Hispanic women and communities across the United States.

The hard work and personal sacrifices of GI Forum leaders, both male and female, finally had their rewards. By 1957, thirteen states had active Forum chapters. In addition to Texas and New Mexico, these included Colorado (1952); Utah (1954); Kansas and Nebraska (1955); California, Michigan, and Missouri (1956); and Arizona, Illinois, Indiana, and Wyoming (1957).[22] By the mid-1960s, the Forum's national membership exceeded 100,000 individuals, with additional chapters forming in Wisconsin, Pennsylvania, Iowa, Oklahoma, Nevada, and Minnesota (1958); Idaho, New York, and Oregon (1959); and West Virginia and Washington, D. C. (1962). [23] In the following decades, Florida and Tennessee (1968), Washington (1969), Arkansas (1970), Connecticut and Maryland (1972), and Virginia (1977) would also see the development of active Forum chapters;[24] and national Forum membership would increase to more than 150,000 individuals.[25]

In the end, of course, Hector García, Vicente Ximenes, and other organizational luminaries were credited with propelling the GI Forum into national prominence. But they were merely the most highlighted agents of the Forum's expansion. At the base of the organizational hierarchy were growing numbers of committed Forumeers, from across the country, whose involvement and interests truly fueled the Forum's development. It was their individual and cooperative efforts that finally brought to fruition the commendable efforts of those at the organization's head. It was also their will and needs that helped the Forum to turn from an agenda concerned solely with veterans' advocacy to important, new areas as the group entered the 1950s—education, civil rights, and economic and employment opportunity.

An American GI Forum float at a Veterans Day parade in Dodge City, Kansas. The AGIF motto, "Education is our freedom and freedom should be everybody's business," indicates the emphasis the Forum has always placed on learning as a means to social betterment. From the group's early days, local chapters organized back-to-school drives, attendance campaigns, and scholarship programs, while the national worked through legal channels for equal educational opportunity.

Photo: Dr. Hector P. García Papers; Special Collections and Archives, Bell Library, Texas A&M University-Corpus Christi.

Flag-raising ceremony jointly sponsored by the Forum and the Daughters of the American Revolution (DAR) at AGIF national headquarters in Albuquerque, New Mexico. When, in February of 1957, a Colorado DAR official disparaged the notion of "Mexican boys" carrying the American flag, a nationwide outcry resulted. U. S. Senator Dennis Chavez responded that "576 'Mexicans' were among those carrying the flag at Bataan . . . What makes you think they can't carry it just as proudly in Colorado?"

Photo: Dr. Hector P. García Papers; Special Collections and Archives, Bell Library, Texas A&M University-Corpus Christi.

Founding president Hector P. García *(at center, beneath eagle)* is greeted by California members of the American GI Forum in 1958. From its beginnings in Corpus Christi, Texas, in 1948, the Forum spread rapidly. By a decade later, there were active chapters in thirteen states; soon afterwards, individual membership would exceed 100,000.

Photo: Dr. Hector P. García Papers; Special Collections and Archives, Bell Library, Texas A&M University-Corpus Christi.

"Viva Kennedy" clubs gave many Mexican Americans their first taste of involvement with the U. S. political process. Immediately flanking presidential nominee John F. Kennedy at a 1960 campaign event are Henry B. González, later a U. S. Representative from San Antonio (*right*), and Dr. Hector P. García (*left*).

Photo: Dr. Hector P. García Papers; Special Collections and Archives, Bell Library, Texas A&M University-Corpus Christi.

U. S. Attorney General Robert F. Kennedy arrives in Chicago to speak at the American GI Forum's 1963 national convention. Many Hispanic Americans had been disappointed by the Justice Department's failure to actively challenge civil-rights violations, and RFK promised that a second term for his brother would bring greater reforms. The task instead fell to Lyndon Johnson.

Photo: Dr. Hector P. García Papers; Special Collections and Archives, Bell Library, Texas A&M University-Corpus Christi.

In a light moment at the 1963 national convention in Chicago, Bobby Kennedy poses with various state contestants for the title of Miss American GI Forum.

Photo: Dr. Hector P. García Papers; Special Collections and Archives, Bell Library, Texas A&M University-Corpus Christi.

Even in a predominantly male organization such as the Forum, women have always played an essential and important role. Many community-service programs and voter-registration drives were run by veterans' spouses and family members. Women also sustained these activities through fundraisers such as barbecues, *tamaladas,* beauty contests, and dances. Shown here at the 1963 Chicago convention are (*front row, left to right*) members Jean Alvarado, Josephine Vera, Alice Alvarado; (*back row, left to right*) Louise Garcia, Consuelo Perez, Betty Maravilla, and Lillian Hernandez.

Photo: Chicago American GI Forum.

Dr. Hector Pérez García meets with President Lyndon Baines Johnson at the White House in 1967. Johnson had firmly established himself as a friend of the American GI Forum back in 1949 with the infamous Felix Longoria incident in Three Rivers, Texas; and many of the reforms Mexican Americans had hoped for with the election of Jack Kennedy actually came to pass under Johnson. LBJ also appointed García to serve in the U. S. delegation to the United Nations.

Photo: Dr. Hector P. García Papers; Special Collections and Archives, Bell Library, Texas A&M University-Corpus Christi.

On June 9, 1967, President Johnson appointed Forum veteran Vicente Ximenes as both a commissioner on the Equal Employment Opportunity Commission and chairman of the (newly created) Inter-Agency Cabinet Committee on Mexican-American Affairs. That October, Johnson visited El Paso, where the committee held a mammoth series of hearings. Although these were boycotted by militant Chicano activists, many participants felt that the hearings resulted in increased awareness of Hispanic social concerns.

Photo: Dr. Hector P. García Papers; Special Collections and Archives, Bell Library, Texas A&M University-Corpus Christi.

The Texas GI Forum's June 1966 march from the Rio Grande Valley to the state capitol in Austin, in support of the United Farm Workers (UFW) and minimum-wage legislation for farm workers. At the head of the march are Dr. Clotilde García, an unidentified farm worker (*holding sign*), the Reverend James Navarro, and Dr. Hector García.

Photo: Dr. Hector P. García Papers; Special Collections and Archives, Bell Library, Texas A&M University-Corpus Christi.

American GI Forum participants in an Independence Day parade; Corpus Christi, Texas, 1968. The Forum's basis as an association of veterans has always commanded respect for its aims even when other, similar organizations were viewed by broader U. S. society as being potentially "subversive."

Photo: Gift of Ernesto Meza; Dr. Hector P. García Papers; Special Collections and Archives, Bell Library, Texas A&M University-Corpus Christi.

The Robstown, Texas, Ladies Auxiliary chapter of the GI Forum. In an era in which many organizations rely upon high technology, lobbying pressure, and sophisticated marketing techniques, one remarkable and continuing strength of the Forum has been its volunteer spirit. Dedicated chapters such as the Robstown group—conspicuously active in local functions such as banquets, funerals, and community-service programs throughout the 1960s and 1970s—have helped to keep the Forum vigorous at the grassroots.

Photo: Dr. Hector P. García Papers; Special Collections and Archives, Bell Library, Texas A&M University-Corpus Christi.

Governor William P. (Bill) Clements of Texas addresses a national youth conference of the American GI Forum in Dallas, 1981. One great concern of the Forum in recent years, when the armed services have become less publicly visible, has been attracting and involving the burgeoning Hispanic youth population into its membership.

Photo: Henry A. J. Ramos.

U. S. Senator Orrin Hatch (R-Utah) meets with American GI Forum chairman José Cano (*left*) and Veterans Outreach Program (VOP) director Carlos Martínez (*right*) in 1982. Cano, regarded by some other civil-rights leaders as a brash and abrasive upstart, nonetheless forged alliances with such important Washington figures as Hatch and Sen. John Tower (R-Texas) to keep Hispanic-American concerns and viewpoints before the Reagan administration.

Photo: Henry A. J. Ramos.

American GI Forum chairman José Cano meets with U. S. Senate majority leader Bob Dole (R-Kansas), himself a decorated World War II veteran. Cano sought to find common ground with Washington leaders in the early 1980s on issues such as veterans' affairs, education, and business and economic development; at the same time, he reached out to the private sector for corporate support and advice.

Photo: Henry A. J. Ramos.

American GI Forum chairman José Cano, Ronald Reagan, and Dr. Hector P. García salute the American flag from the dais of the Forum's August 1983 national convention in El Paso. Much like LBJ's visit to the same city some fifteen years earlier, President Reagan's very presence in El Paso would be a source of displeasure for some. The following year, however, Reagan would award Dr. García the Presidential Medal of Freedom—the highest honor the president can bestow upon a civilian—for meritorious public service.

Photo: Ronald Reagan Presidential Library.

Chapter 3

Education Reform

In its formative years the GI Forum adopted the motto, "Education Is our Freedom and Freedom Should Be Everybody's Business." From the beginning, education was an area of principal concern to the organization. There were many important reasons for this. Mexican Americans' second-class status was traditionally attributed to low levels of educational achievement. In Texas, for example, Mexican-American children averaged a mere 3.5 years of formal schooling during the Forum's early years, compared to more than ten years for Anglo children. Circumstances in other states with large Mexican-American populations were not much better and would not improve for many years to come. According to 1960 Census data, Mexican-American students in the key southwestern states of Arizona, California, and Colorado recorded markedly lower levels of education attainment than both Anglo and black students.[1] With so little education, Mexican-Americans were largely relegated to base labor and the lower end of the socioeconomic spectrum.

Supporting all of this was a long-standing and widespread culture of segregation that discouraged Mexican-American educational achievement in both formal and informal ways. Historian David Montejano in his book *Anglos and Mexicans in the Making of Texas, 1836-1986* recounts statements of Anglo leaders in south Texas, originally recorded by the noted social scientist Paul S. Taylor:

> Repulsion was evident in the response to Taylor's questions about "mixing with Mexicans." As one Nueces County farmer put it: "I don't believe in mixing. They are filthy and lousy . . . I have raised my two children with the idea that they are above the doggone Mexican nationality and I believe a man should." A. H. Divinney, superintendent of Aguas Dulces schools in the same county, explained that Anglos "would drop dead if you mentioned mixing Mexicans with whites. They would rather not have an education themselves than associate with these dirty Mexicans." Several counties away in Dimmit a school official noted that such intense opinions were commonplace: "There would be a revolution in the community if Mexicans wanted to come to white schools. Sentiment is bitterly against it. It is based on racial inferiority."

Such sentiments permeated Anglo society and institutions to the point that many Mexican Americans themselves questioned their intellectual equality to whites or the wisdom of pursuing education beyond the early grades, when employment became a viable option.[2]

The Forum's response to all of this was two-fold. On one hand, GI Forums sought to develop local strategies to promote greater educational interest and performance among Mexican-American youth in communities where they operated. Mainly this was accomplished through grassroots community education and support initiatives, such as town hall meetings, neighborhood-based pro-education campaigns, and youth scholarship programs.

On the other hand, Forum leaders were well aware that the principal cause of low education attainment among Mexican Americans was not lack of interest in education, but rather systematic barriers to equal opportunity: widespread segregation, racially disparate school financing, and culturally and linguistically biased performance evaluation measures. Given this understanding, Forum efforts in the education realm were increasingly focused on system reform. Generally, these efforts involved Forum legal and political challenges to local school districts and education officials.

In its initial endeavors to promote education, the GI Forum showed itself to be both a uniting and innovative force within Mexican-American communities. Invariably, among the first orders of business for local Forum chapters was the establishment of a full-time education committee. Each committee formed partnerships with other community organizations, such as the League of United Latin American Citizens

(LULAC), to support pro-education strategies such as "back-to-school" drives and attendance campaigns. Mexican-American families were informed about the essential role of formal education in their children's lives by way of door-to-door visits, written materials, bumper stickers, and spots on local radio stations.

In the late 1950s, the Forum played a large role in assisting LULAC in developing an innovative preschool program called the "Little Schools of 400." These were community-supported preschools that taught basic English to children from non-English-speaking homes. The program produced impressive results: 95 percent of its participants entered public schools at the same reading level as English-speaking children.[3] The success of the Little Schools of 400 program encouraged the Texas legislature to fund similar programs and later inspired the federally funded Operation Headstart program for preschool youngsters. Díaz de Cossío, *et al.* place the Forum's contributions to this work in the context of Mexican-American organizational impulses following World War II, which highlighted a special sense of urgency to improve community educational conditions:

> Motivated by veterans, new organizations like the American GI Forum emerged . . . Conscious of the urgent need to gain more adequate education for the Spanish-speaking population, they created the so-called "Little Schools of 400," whose principal objective was to teach pre-school children the 400 most commonly used English words, with the idea of facilitating their educational success . . . One of this effort's main motivations was to sensitize the North American education system to the particular needs of this population, which were not being addressed in an adequate way . . .

Ensuring the success of these undertakings required considerable ancillary work in organizing fundraising events and sponsorship activities, such as dances, *tamaladas*, and local business solicitations.[4] Support for these efforts was generally widespread due to the perseverance and commitment of Forumeers and other community leaders; and the result was a heightened consciousness of the critical importance of education. In most areas, enrollment and retention of *mexicano* school children increased in the lower grades during the years following the initiation of back-to-school drives and other pro-education campaigns. Unfortunately, these improvements were not alone enough to change the longer-term educational and economic prospects of most Mexican-American families. Beyond the improvements they brought, there remained larger structural barriers to equal educational opportunity.

Throughout the Southwest (and particularly in Texas) Mexican-American school children were blatantly segregated in "Mexican" schools with outdated programs and dilapidated facilities, much the way blacks were segregated in schools in the South. Although Mexican Americans were legally characterized as white under the prevailing "separate but equal" doctrine, widespread Spanish monolingualism in many Mexican-American households led Anglo administrators to justify Mexican-American exclusion from educational programs and facilities attended by white, English-speaking children. Generally, Anglo school officials claimed that segregating Mexican-American children in all "Mexican" schools facilitated their acculturation to mainstream society. But, more often than not, the outcome was to deny Mexican Americans the same educational opportunities and social standing afforded to whites. According to Joan W. Moore,

> The physically segregated school was a natural reflection of the prevailing belief in Mexican racial inferiority. No Southwestern state upheld legally the segregation of Mexican-American children, yet the practice was widespread. Separate schools were built and maintained, in theory, simply because of residential segregation or to benefit the Mexican child. He had a "language handicap" and needed to be "Americanized" before mixing with Anglo children. His presence in an integrated school . . . would hinder the progress of white American children.[5]

To challenge such segregation in unequal schools, the GI Forum began in the early 1950s to support a series of legal and political challenges to local school districts and education officials in Texas. In all, between 1950 and 1960, the Forum filed nearly one hundred formal complaints challenging school desegregation and other educational inequities. This process took the organization to the state's highest decision-making branches, and its successes in these realms brought positive changes for Mexican Americans in Texas and elsewhere.

The notion of exacting educational improvements through the courts did not occur to GI Forum leaders in a vacuum. As early as 1930, Chicano attorneys representing parents in Del Rio, Texas, had employed the "separate but equal" legal doctrine pertaining to "white" and "negro" facilities to argue that school officials there were arbitrarily and illegally depriving Mexican-American students of facilities available to "other white races" in the same school system.[6] Contending that the plaintiffs were segregated solely because of their Mexican ancestry, attorneys in *Independent School District v. Salvatierra*[7] demanded the end of such discriminatory action by Del Rio officials. Del Rio's attorneys justified the segregation of Mexican-American students on the basis of language deficiencies, which they argued required local discretionary authority to employ remedial interventions, including separate schools, by public school administrators. The trial court, however, agreed with Salvatierra's lawyers and granted an injunction against the separation of *mexicano* and Anglo children within the school system. On review, however, the Texas Court of Civil Appeals reversed the decision and voided the injunction. While confirming that arbitrary segregation of Mexican-American children was unlawful, the court ruled that absent proof of intent to discriminate, segregation of Spanish surname students in separate campuses due to pedagogical considerations was not an unreasonable exercise of local school authority. Thus, correction of language deficiencies as determined by Del Rio school administrators was deemed adequate justification for separation.

Ten years after the *Salvatierra* ruling, LULAC initiated an administrative action against the Ozona, Texas, school board, charging that district with arbitrary and illegal segregation.[8] In deciding the case, the Texas superintendent of public schools ruled that "under the laws of the state, children of [Mexican-American] extraction are classified as white and therefore have a right to attend Anglo American schools in the communities in which they live."[9] The ruling did not, however, question the legitimacy of local school officials separating Mexican-American and Anglo students in the same or different schools on the basis of administratively determined English-language deficiencies in the *mexicano* population.

Thus, while the *Salvatierra* and Ozona rulings clearly set precedents indicting arbitrary segregation, each ruling left open important loopholes which allowed school officials and locales to circumvent the law. In most school districts, therefore, *mexicano* students continued to be segregated in separate and unequal schools; and in those cases where Mexican-American and Anglo children attended the same schools, *de facto* segregation continued as Mexican-American students were tracked into separate classrooms and inferior educational programs.[10]

In 1946, California's southern district court ruled in *Mendez v. Westminster*[11] that school districts in that state were segregating Mexican Americans from Anglo students on the basis of ethnic characteristics alone. The practice was ruled unconstitutional, since in the court's opinion under U. S. and California law segregation of Spanish-speaking or other non-English ancestry public school children could only legally obtain where indiscriminate examination of such students' language and learning capacities established a pedagogical rationale for differential treatment.[12] The ninth circuit court of appeals upheld the lower court ruling, but added a theoretical layer to the problem of Mexican-American segregation.[13] It found that California school districts were segregating under color of law, even though segregation of Mexican-Americans was not provided for by state law. Segregation, it said, was allowed in California only as to certain excepted ancestries and conditions stipulated by state law. Because Mexican Americans were not among these legally enumerated exceptions, their placement in separate public schools as a matter of course was unconstitutional. In effect, Mexican-American students were to be treated legally as members of the white race. Since Texas, like California, had no state law requiring segregation of Mexican-American children, yet practiced segregation extensively, Gus García, the talented young attorney who would later represent the GI Forum, felt the *Mendez* decision provided ample artillery for a revival of Chicano efforts to challenge the legality of Texas school policy.

To test his theory, García sought from Texas attorney general Price Daniel a formal clarification of his positions relative to Texas and U. S. segregation laws. In a written exchange with the attorney general, García held segregation for Mexican Americans to be permissible only when separation was due to language deficiencies based on "scientific" tests applied to all students regardless of racial ancestry.[14] Daniel affirmed García's position:

> I am certainly pleased to know that your interpretation of this . . . agrees with ours . . . The law prohibits discrimination against or segregation of Latin Americans on account of race or descent, and the law permits no subterfuge to accomplish such discrimination.[15]

In fact, Mexican-American children in numerous Texas school districts were being segregated on the basis of ethnicity alone. Through the emergent work of University of Texas academics George I. Sánchez and Virgil E. Strickland, García could document numerous districts in which standardized testing of educational aptitude was lacking or applied only to Mexican-American children.[16] Moreover, Sánchez's and Strickland's studies documented the use of various administrative strategies to perpetuate Mexican-American segregation in Texas schools. Some districts, for example, were gerrymandered into separate "zones" that confined all Spanish-speaking children to one zone and all Anglo children to the other. Other districts established "freedom of choice" plans, which enabled a small number of Mexican-American children to attend Anglo schools but only Mexican-American children to enroll in "Mexican" schools.[17]

On the basis of Price Daniel's interpretation and Sánchez's and Strickland's studies, García in 1947 brought wrongful discrimination suits on behalf of Minerva Delgado and twenty other Mexican-American families against the Bastrop, Elgin, Martindale, and Travis Independent School Districts of south Texas.[18] Arguing before the U. S. district court and its presiding judge, Ben H. Rice, Jr., García contended that because Mexican-American students were segregated in the respective districts without objective testing for skill deficiencies, they were being treated as a "class apart" from the mainstream white community. In this way, according to García, such students were being illegally deprived of equal facilities, services, and educational instruction.[19]

The argument succeeded. In a judgment rendered on June 15, 1948, Rice found that the defendant school districts had unlawfully discriminated against Mexican-American students under federal law. According to Rice,

> The regulations, customs, usages, and practices of the defendants, Bastrop ISD of Bastrop County, *et al.,* in so far as they or any of them have segregated pupils of Mexican or Latin American descent in separate classes and schools within the respective school districts heretofore set out, and each of them is, arbitrary and discriminatory and in violation of plaintiffs' constitutional rights as guaranteed by the Fourteenth Amendment to the Constitution of the United States, and are illegal.[20]

The judge went on to permanently enjoin the designated districts from continued segregation of Mexican-American children, reminding district officials that such children were entitled to the same facilities and services enjoyed by Anglo children of the state.[21]

In another part of the judgment, Rice enjoined Texas school superintendent L. A. Woods from participating in or otherwise perpetuating the segregation of Mexican-American schoolchildren. Woods dutifully complied with the order, reporting to all Texas school districts that under state and federal law separate education could be continued for black students only, a practice that would soon lose official sanction with the 1954 U. S. Supreme Court ruling in *Brown v. Board of Education of Topeka, Kansas.* In a written memorandum to each district, Woods listed the central points of Judge Rice's various holdings in *Delgado.* He also informed the districts that he would take necessary action to ensure that the court's directives were obeyed.[22]

Clearly, *Delgado* was both unprecedented and highly significant. Consequently, Mexican-American civil rights leaders, including Dr. Hector García, George I. Sánchez, and Gus García believed the ruling would tangibly improve schooling opportunities for Texas children of Mexican descent—and, logically, it should have. But, like the rulings in the *Salvatierra* and Ozona cases of previous years, the judgment allowed school districts to maintain separate classes for Mexican-American and Anglo students on the same campus for the first grade, where separation could be based on standardized evaluations of all children's instructional needs.[23] In addition, the school districts were given a period of nearly a year and a half to comply with the judgment.[24] In essence, then, owing to built-in biases in the state's all-English language evaluation system, *Delgado* accepted the concept of substantial Mexican-American segregation in the first grade. Furthermore, Rice's judgment granted school districts ample time both to avoid affirmative compliance and to design a series of strategies to perpetuate *mexicano* segregation after the court-imposed compliance date. For a time, various school systems did successfully establish such new strategies, despite their frequently absurd rationales.

Because *Delgado* permitted segregation of Mexican Americans only in the first grade for language deficiencies determined by testing, for example, many school districts developed special first grade programs for the "language deficient." Several districts offered these special first-grade programs on a multi-year basis. Mexican-American children were highly over-represented in these programs. Typically, such students would be tested and placed for one year in a "low first" grade program and then moved (without further testing) in the second year (normally second grade) to a "high first" grade program. The development of such schemes kept Mexican-American students in them from completing the normal first- and second-grade tracks offered to Anglo youngsters of the same age. In some cases, Mexican-American students were retained in such extended first grade programs for as many as three years.[25] Furthermore, in direct contravention of *Delgado*, many Texas school districts did not apply testing or alternative placement policies to white students; and some districts even segregated Mexican-American pupils who spoke *only* English.

Certain Texas school districts simply did not recognize *Delgado*. In Del Rio, for example, a "freedom of choice" plan was left virtually unchanged following the *Delgado* ruling, notwithstanding forceful efforts by GI Forum leaders to document its unlawful effects on Mexican-American rights and opportunities.[26] Similar recalcitrance was characteristic of school districts in Robestown, George West, Mathis, Orange Grove, Bishop, Driscoll, Sinton, Three Rivers, Encinal, Beeville, and Rio Hondo.

Convinced of the *Delgado* ruling's moral call to end Texas school segregation, yet equally aware of the need to push beyond the ruling's limits, Hector García and other GI Forum leaders took to the forefront efforts to realize equal educational opportunity for Mexican-Americans in Texas and elsewhere.[27] Working in late 1948 with George I. Sánchez and various LULAC affiliates on follow-ups to Sánchez's school segregation studies, Dr. García headed numerous onsite Forum inspections of south Texas school districts, visiting classes, conducting interviews, taking photographs, and preparing detailed reports of unlawful segregation practices. These site investigations strategically positioned Forum and other Mexican-American community leaders to hold school districts accountable to *Delgado*.

Because state school superintendent Woods' compliance memorandum to local districts indicated *Delgado* would be honored through state enforcement, Forumeer Cris Alderete filed a complaint against the Del Rio school system in January of 1949 to challenge its blatant and unlawful continuation of Mexican-American segregation. A state investigator responding to Alderete's complaint recorded the following striking evidence of such segregation by Del Rio officials:

> Two school campuses were separated by railroad tracks. The north elementary school campus was reserved strictly for Anglo children, although zoned for all students in an area where many Mexican-American children lived. The south campus had four buildings, two of which had *mexicano* students only.

As in other districts of the region, moreover, physical conditions at the schools' facilities significantly favored Anglo students.[28]

Following a review of the investigator's report, superintendent Woods concurred with Alderete's arguments and suspended the Del Rio system's accreditation in February.[29] But Woods' commitment to comply with *Delgado* proved too much, too fast for the Texas legislature. In an "emergency action" the following June, the legislature transferred the powers of the school superintendent's office to a new education commissioner.[30] Woods remained throughout the remainder of his term in office as an advisor to the new commissioner, J. W. Edgar, and then saw his position abolished.[31] Within two months of the legislature's action, Woods' recession of the Del Rio school system's accreditation was voided and the district was reinstated.[32]

The GI Forum responded by passing at its 1949 membership convention a resolution calling for suspension of all federal funds to schools that practiced segregation.[33] The Forum also demanded official investigations of the many school districts Hector García's and George

I. Sánchez's inspections had determined to be in violation of state and federal laws (*ibid.*). Finally, to protest reversal of the Woods decision to suspend Del Rio's school accreditation, GI Forum principals initiated a massive drive in Del Rio's *mexicano* community to enroll Mexican-American children in the town's Anglo school.

Cris Alderete and Hector García co-chaired the Del Rio school enrollment campaign. Driving through Del Rio's *barrios*[34] before the school year's commencement with public-address systems attached to their cars, García, Alderete, and other community leaders urged families to assert their right to equal educational opportunity. When school began in the fall, more than one thousand Chicano children petitioned to enroll in the Anglo school. This eventually forced the district to end its "freedom of choice" program and to build a new facility to accommodate Mexican-American demands for improved educational opportunity.[35]

Despite sporadic local successes of this kind, the need for systemic educational reforms in the larger political and legal contexts remained considerable. The abolition of the state superintendent's office made the GI Forum's task all the greater. In a May 8, 1950, policy statement, the Texas Board of Education decreed that local school boards would be given every opportunity to comply with *Delgado* before complaints of violation could be considered by the state's education commissioner. Accordingly, the board instructed Commissioner Edgar to refrain from determining district compliance in segregation and equity disputes until local efforts to remedy complaints had been exhausted and the attorney general had been consulted to determine appropriate corrective action. Only thereafter would hearing and enforcement authority devolve to the commissioner.[36] In effect, the new state policy required separate and multiple complaint procedures for each of the twenty-two districts the Forum reports listed as violators. For the next three years, Forum and other civil rights advocates did the best they could to work with this cumbersome and highly unfriendly procedure. Not surprisingly, they experienced only modest success.[37]

By late 1954, however, GI Forum attorneys Gus García, James de Anda, and Carlos Cardena developed an alternative strategy: Forum attorneys simply began filing federal lawsuits against districts failing to desegregate in accordance with *Delgado*. Resort to the courts offered numerous advantages. First, the legal process was generally more efficient than administrative appeals. Second, it afforded the opportunity primarily to use facts rather than negotiation in pursuing educational equity. Finally, legal decisions were more effectively binding than administrative rulings. The major difficulty with this strategy was the high cost of sustaining effective legal action; but a deeply determined Forum, and other Mexican-American leaders and groups, provided the necessary support.

Thus, from 1955 to 1957 the GI Forum led a series of suits that substantially undermined continuing efforts by Texas educators to disregard state and federal prohibitions against the segregation of Mexican-American students in public schools. The most prominent of the suits were those brought against the Carrizo Springs and Kingsville Independent School Districts, in 1955; the Mathis Independent School District, in 1956; and the Driscoll Consolidated Independent School District, in 1957.

The Carrizo Springs and Kingsville cases were settled to the Forum's satisfaction after the commencement of litigation resulted in state and local measures designed to improve educational opportunities. In each of these suits the Forum accused the defendant district of administering programs that barred, prohibited, and excluded Mexican-American children solely on the basis of their ethnic origin from attending schools and using facilities maintained exclusively for Anglo students. Forum attorneys contended that local and state school officials had failed to adopt policy reforms required to correct resulting harm to Mexican-American students, notwithstanding continuing good faith efforts by community leaders and others to encourage such action. Because neither the offending districts nor the state afforded due process and equal protection to prevent injury and discrimination resulting from the exclusionary school policies, the Forum argued that Mexican-Americans were being denied rights to which they were entitled under *Delgado* and the Fourteenth Amendment. On June 13, 1955, federal action against the Carrizo Springs Independent School District was dismissed following a formal agreement by the violating district to end segregation of Mexican-American pupils. Forum-sponsored investigations and reports well into the following school year showed that the agreement had resulted in substantial gains for Mexican-American students in the Carrizo Springs school system.[38]

In *Salinas v. Kingsville ISD*, Forum attorneys challenged a district "freedom of choice" scheme that permitted Anglos to choose whether to attend predominantly Mexican-American schools absent a reciprocal extension of choice to Mexican Americans. Despite Gus García's and Carlos Cardena's documentation of unlawful segregation in the district dating back to 1914, education commissioner Edgar had failed to order the district to cease and desist its discriminatory practices.[39] A suit against the district filed in federal court on April 23, 1955, was eventually dismissed when, with the encouragement of the judge, the Kingsville school board agreed to modify its policies to the Forum's satisfaction.

In late 1955, Forum attorneys filed federal suit against the Mathis Independent School District on behalf of Trinidad Villareal and other Mexican-American parents of the district. The suit followed more than five years of the most blatant refusal by district school officials to comply with *Delgado*. Despite the district's obstinance, Commissioner Edgar argued on its behalf during the court proceedings for dismissal of the case on grounds that federal involvement in the matter was "frivolous in concept, nebulous in form, lacking in substance," and otherwise unfounded.[40]

The Forum's suit in *Villareal v. Mathis ISD* was dismissed and an agreed order entered on a technicality.[41] Forum attorneys, however, continued to press for change in Mathis, threatening to file federal suit against Commissioner Edgar and the Texas Education Agency if appropriate action was not taken. In response, Edgar ordered Mathis school officials to cease and desist the district's arbitrary retention and segregation of Mexican-American pupils for two years in the first grade. He also ordered the district to comply with *Delgado* in the upper grades.[42] When the district failed to fully comply, Edgar revoked its accreditation. To regain accreditation district officials had to close previously "Mexican-American" facilities and integrate classrooms. Notwithstanding these changes, 60 percent of the district's Mexican-American students remained completely segregated in Mathis, but the victory was significant for the mid-1950s. Indeed, *Villareal v. Mathis*

ISD marked a beginning of the end for extended first-grade programs to perpetuate Chicano segregation.

The 1957 Forum-supported suit in *Hernández v. Driscoll Consolidated Independent School District* constituted the Forum's most significant contribution to the advancement of Chicano educational rights and opportunities.[43] The Forum's suit charged that Mexican-American students in Driscoll were segregated in an extended, three-year first grade program. School personnel argued that the children were placed according to language deficiencies determined by standardized testing, but trial testimony later revealed that testing was conducted only at the outset of the first school year, with students remaining segregated thereafter regardless of their English-language proficiency. In at least one instance, a Mexican-American child was shown to have been tracked into a "Mexican" first grade program despite the fact that she spoke *no* Spanish. Only after the services of an attorney were secured by her parents to challenge the district's policy was the child allowed to participate in an Anglo section of her school, making her the first Mexican-American student so placed in the local superintendent's twelve-year tenure there.[44]

Finding for the plaintiffs, Judge James V. Allred held that Driscoll school authorities had determined placement of pupils "not only for beginners, but through the first and second grades, not on a basis of individual aptitudes or attainments, but against all children of Latin American extraction as a class." On this basis, Allred concluded, the Driscoll grouping of separate classes was arbitrary and unreasonable, and he permanently enjoined and restrained the district from continuing its discriminatory policies.

The effects of the Driscoll case were once and for all to deny the legal legitimacy of multi-year first-grade programs for Mexican-American children and to make unlawful the segregation of such children absent uniform, standardized testing.

These legal developments set the stage for corollary legal gains by Mexican-Americans during coming decades in cases such as *Cisneros v. Corpus Christi Independent School District* (in which the federal district court for southern Texas ruled that "Mexican-Americans are 'an identifiable ethnic minority group' for the purpose of school desegregation"); *U. S. v. Texas*[45] (which ordered Texas school authorities to take affirmative steps to compel local and state compliance with Mexican-American and other minority rights under federal law and the U. S. Constitution); and *Keyes v. Denver* (in which local school authorities were ordered to implement bilingual-bicultural programs for Spanish-speaking children of the district). Beyond these contributions to Mexican-American advancement, the Forum's successful advocacy efforts in the education arena during its formative years inspired new confidence in Mexican Americans everywhere to challenge continuing discrimination and injustice whenever and wherever they found it.

The strategies of the Forum did not themselves reverse the blatant barriers to equality of educational opportunity that had historically been placed before Mexican Americans. In fact, initially, little changed on the face of Mexican-American education in American society. As recently as 1968, for example, 66 percent of all Mexican-American students in Texas still attended racially identifiable schools, with 40 percent of those enrolled in schools whose student bodies were over 80 percent Chicano and almost 21 percent attending schools whose student bodies were over 90 percent minority.[46] Furthermore, a 1972 U. S. Commission on Civil Rights report describes the condition of education for most Southwest Mexican-Americans as being not much different than it had been in 1948.[47]

Notwithstanding these persistent problems, it cannot be denied that early Forum activities helped significantly to undermine long-standing official justifications for Chicano segregation in Texas and other states. And these efforts in turn made possible subsequent gains for Hispanic Americans in later decades. The GI Forum's work to challenge the unequal education of Mexican-Americans during the late 1940s and the 1950s warrants enduring recognition and appreciation.

Chapter 4

Early Struggles for Justice and Equal Opportunity

The GI Forum's attention to educational issues was a logical extension of its broader concern for Hispanic civil rights. In each state and locality into which the Forum expanded, chapters played an increasingly active role in combating such traditional forms of injustice as police brutality, public discrimination, labor exploitation, and voter-rights infringement. As was the case in the Forum's educational battles, early gains in civil rights were not always markedly evident. Generally, Forum-inspired changes were greatest on a local or regional level; but these changes were no less significant to those who benefited from them.

Los Angeles' celebrated Sleepy Lagoon incident strongly reflects the general level of mistreatment to which Mexican Americans were subjected at this time. On August 2, 1942, a Chicano youth named Jose Díaz was found beaten to death on a dirt road on the outskirts of the city. No weapon was found, but Díaz had taken part in a gang clash the preceding evening at a nearby swimming hole, and an autopsy showed his death had resulted from a skull fracture. In the fall, twenty-two members of the Chicano 38th Street Gang were charged in the crime. According to the prosecution every defendant was chargeable with Díaz's murder. According to this logic, the twenty-two youths were tied together on sixty-six charges.

Judge Charles W. Fricke oversaw the trial. Fricke made little secret of his bias against Mexican-Americans and permitted numerous irregularities in the proceedings. A report from the grand jury investigation by the Los Angeles Police Department citing the "inherently criminal and violent" tendencies of Aztec descendants was permitted as evidence against the accused.[1] The defendants were not allowed to bathe or to shave before entering the courtroom, which undoubtedly created a bad impression for jury members. Witnesses provided ample testimony indicating the defendants were not involved in the deceased's death. The prosecution failed to repudiate this testimony or to prove any evidence of criminal agreement or conspiracy. Nevertheless, in January, 1943, sentences were passed down for each of the defendants, ranging from assault to first-degree murder. The decision was ultimately reversed through the efforts of a Sleepy Lagoon Defense Committee headed by noted scholar and community advocate Carey McWilliams, but not before two and a half years of the defendants' youth had been spent imprisoned under false charges.[2]

The Sleepy Lagoon case incited considerable anti-Hispanic sentiment in southern California and elsewhere. The Los Angeles press, including the *L.A. Times* and the Hearst newspapers, exploited the situation with sensationalist journalism, emphasizing an alleged Mexican-American "crime wave." Such reporting both pressured and encouraged local police departments to engage in systematic arrests of supposed Mexican-American gang members, typically identified by their zoot suit clothing and *pachuco* hair styles. Police also beat and otherwise harassed Mexican-American youth.

In April and May 1943, some minor altercations took place between zoot-suiters and Anglo military personnel in Los Angeles and Oakland. These altercations escalated in the first days of June, when serious clashes broke out between zoot-suited Mexican-American youth and Anglo soldiers and sailors in Los Angeles. Street cars and buses were stopped, and zoot-suiters pulled off; theaters were entered, lights turned on, and zoot-suiters were dragged out by the servicemen. Many were assaulted and had their clothes ripped off and their hair cut. These vicious attacks quickly became virtually an undeclared war on all young Mexican-Americans by roving bands of Anglo servicemen. The conflict reached a peak on June 7, when fleets of taxis filled with sailors cruised the streets of Los Angeles seeking victims. Police responded by following the cabs at a distance and then arresting *victims* when fighting broke out.

According to Matt S. Meier and Feliciano Ribera,

> What had begun as a series of street brawls quickly turned into a full-fledged race riot incited by the press and condoned or ignored by major law enforcement agencies. Rioting also broke out in Pasadena, Long Beach, and San Diego. This violence triggered similar racial attacks against Mexican-Americans in Chicago, Detroit, and Philadelphia during the summer of 1943. Throughout the country there was strong reaction to these outrages, and *Time* magazine later called the Los Angeles violence "the ugliest brand of mob action since the coolie race riots of the 1870s."

A citizens committee appointed by Governor Earl Warren to investigate the riots found that, while their causes were complex, they were principally "the result of racial antagonism stimulated by inflammatory news reporting and discriminatory police practices."

Such blatant disregard for the civil rights of Mexican Americans was aggravated by the growing illegal immigration and undocumented residence of impoverished Mexican citizens seeking economic opportunity in the United States. The presence of such individuals as cheap laborers in agriculture and industry created complex economic, social, and political tensions in the Southwest and Midwest, which were the main recipients of Mexican labor influx.

Businesses employing undocumented workers clearly benefited from their availability. Not only did the willingness of these workers to produce for exceptionally poor wages sustain lower production costs and proportionately higher profits, their status as illegal immigrants made them docile out of fear of deportation, and consequently they were easily exploited. Anglo workers, displaced by cheaper Mexican labor, along with racist elements of mainstream society, predictably resented the illegal immigrant's presence in their communities. Mexican immigrants were commonly labeled "wetbacks" by Anglos, referring to the widespread notion of immigrants swimming across the Rio Grande River to avoid detection and deportation by the U. S. border patrol. They were also subjected to especially severe social controls. According to Montejano,

> The laboring class was seen not only as inferior but also as untouchable . . . physical separation was necessary . . . elaborate social rules . . . defined the proper place and modes of defer-

ences . . . designed to make sure Mexicans understood their inferior status in the social order.[3]

In addition, then, to the economic exploitation Mexican immigrants experienced, they were equally subjected to supporting social injustice. Invariably, these circumstances carried negative ramifications for Americans of Mexican descent, who were frequently perceived and treated by Anglos as "immigrants."

During World War II these problems were exacerbated by the establishment of the Bracero Program, which legally brought 200,000 Mexican laborers to the United States to assist American agricultural interests claiming war-related labor shortages.[4] The *bracero* workforce was concentrated in cotton, sugar beets, fruits, and vegetables, and in some areas comprised the bulk of the unskilled labor for these crops. After the war the program was retained and expanded, despite the return to the workforce of millions of Americans from overseas service duty. In fact, between 1951 and 1959 the number of *braceros*[5] employed each year by U. S. agriculture more than doubled, reaching more than 445,000 in 1956.

The legal presence of *braceros* masked the growing use and exploitation of illegal Mexican immigrants by both agricultural and industrial employers during America's postwar years of rapid economic expansion. The economic hardships for Mexican workers in their own country were such that they were pushed by the hundreds of thousands to enter the United States. Mexican workers were also pulled to the United States by American employers eager to hire them. This push-pull factor produced an ample supply of illegal laborers upon which American business could depend to sustain a low-wage, nonstriking workforce.

According to labor historian Kitty Calavita,

> In 1943, approximately 12,000 illegal immigrants were apprehended; by 1945, the number had jumped to almost 70,000. By the end of this period, the gap between apprehensions and legal braceros was widening rapidly. In 1949, when there were 107,000 braceros, the INS apprehended slightly over twice that many undocumented workers. Two years later, the ratio was 3 to 1.[6]

Mexican-American workers were pitted against their *mexicano* counterparts for opportunities in the job market. The conflict this created pushed down wages and working conditions. A 1951 Bureau of Agricultural Economics report acknowledged that *bracero* wages did not consistently meet mandated minimum levels, hours worked were typically misreported in favor of employers, payments to workers were delayed, and worker housing and food provisions frequently failed to meet minimum legal requirements.[7] In 1950, some Mexican-American farm workers in California were actually paid less than *braceros*. During the same year in Texas, farmers in the Rio Grande Valley paid pickers $1.25 per hundred pounds of product, with many farmers paying as little as 50 to 75 cents. The national average was $2.45 per hundred pounds.

When U. S. unions protested these practices on behalf of organized labor, government officials claimed a desire to limit the entry of Mexican workers in accordance with American immigration laws and the *bracero* accord. But, through cyclical omissions of state action and enforcement, government policy maintained a revolving door that allowed Mexicans to enter the United States at will when it was to the advantage of business. Business, on the other hand, stated its desire to hire American workers, but claimed that Americans were unwilling to perform the work done by Mexicans. Political considerations compounded the economic imperatives to maintain the revolving door to and from Mexico's cheap labor supply. In Texas, for example, Harry S. Truman depended heavily on the state's *bracero*-dependent ranchers and farmers to secure his narrow election victory in 1948; and the ranch of Governor Allan Shivers was reportedly one of the state's largest employers of illegal Mexican labor.

Complicating the situation still further for *mexicanos* were countervailing social, political, and economic pressures to clamp down on illegal immigration. During 1949-1950, for example, the United States experienced an economic recession that inspired many Americans, conservatives and liberals alike, to decry employment of non-citizens. Responding to these pressures, the U. S. Border Patrol initiated a drive to apprehend and deport "illegals" that extended into Mexican-American communities throughout the West. Carey McWilliams wrote,

> The viciousness of the present roundup consists in the fact that
> once such a campaign has been decreed, there is only one way to
> carry it into effect; namely to make systematic house-to-house raids
> in every Mexican settlement . . . The mere announcement that the
> Immigration Service is conducting a roundup of this character oper-
> ates, of course, to spread fear and panic . . . [8]

One year later, with the advent of significant United States troop
involvement in the Korean conflict, demand for cheap foreign labor
rebounded. The availability of jobs renewed the flow of Mexican
undocumented laborers northward. However, the end of the Korean
War brought another recession, beginning in 1953. Coinciding with the
rise of McCarthyism and growing anti-foreigner sentiment,[9] the recession of 1953-1955 informed a new wave of anti-immigrant initiative
and political injustice against *mexicanos.*

Citing concern over possible illegal entry into the United States of
political subversives from Mexico and elsewhere, U. S. Attorney
General Herbert Brownell, Jr. announced a new immigration policy in
June 1954, designed to facilitate mass deportations of "illegals."
Immigration Service director Joseph M. Swing implemented the new
policy, now known infamously as "Operation Wetback." Between 1953
and 1956, "Operation Wetback" deported more than two million people. Touted in the media as the solution to "the illegal problem," the
drive was often merciless and abusive.

To many it appeared to be a contradiction that, on the one hand, the
INS was deporting "wetbacks" while, on the other hand, thousands of
braceros were being allowed to enter and work in the United States.
According to Chicano activist Bert Corona, however,

> What was concerning the INS, in league with the agricultural
> industry and other employers of *braceros,* was that *braceros* were
> protesting their poor working and living conditions and that numbers
> of them were skipping out on their contracts and moving into cities
> to find work without documents. Hence, Operation Wetback was
> really . . . meant to scare the *braceros* into remaining in their camps
> and accepting their conditions and, in this way, to preserve the
> revolving door of reserve surplus labor from Mexico.[10]

The significance of all this for *mexicanos* is that it entrenched them
in a position of relative powerlessness and compromise. Tolerating circumstances as they were meant accepting criminally low wages and

punishing work conditions. Challenging these injustices, however, meant risking the possibility of job loss, defaming accusations of subversiveness, and deportation (sometimes notwithstanding U. S. citizenship).[11] In fact, the very nature of Mexican immigration and exploitation in American society undermined the fundamental rights of the *mexicano* people. For any number of social, political, or economic reasons, persons of Mexican ancestry could be unjustly but legally subjected to official action and intimidation; and throughout the late 1940s and the 1950s they were.

Few Mexican-American groups were able to effectively challenge civil rights violations of this sort, or those otherwise related to *mexicano* labor exploitation, discrimination, and political manipulation. Anti-foreign sentiments during the Joseph McCarthy era were at a high pitch, and many Mexican-American organizations fell silent. However, the GI Forum refused to be silenced. Moreover, the Forum was uniquely positioned to withstand threats of black-listing, investigation, and reprisal.

According to National Council of La Raza president Raúl Yzaguirre, the Forum was the organization best equipped to survive the misguided threats of some anti-communists to its advocacy role due to its patriotic veterans and family composition.[12] Forum critics were hard put to paint the organization as being communist-inspired, given the distinguished service records and demonstrated patriotism of its principal members. Furthermore, Forum leaders were endorsed by influential members of the Catholic church. In New Mexico, an FBI investigation of allegedly subversive Forum activities was ended when the Albuquerque Forum's parish monsignor and archbishop, Edwin Vincent Byrne, defended Forum activities there.[13] Such support was also offered by church principals in Texas, including Archbishop Robert Lucey in San Antonio, Bishop Mariano Garriga in Corpus Christi, and the Forum's actively supportive chaplain, the Rev. Erwin Juraschek.[14] Due to these factors (i.e., a patriotic organizational tenor and church support), the Forum continued to pursue and secure gains for the Mexican-American community when other groups could not; and this propelled the organization into a leading role in the national civil rights arena.

Not surprisingly, civil rights violations associated with the growing presence of Mexican workers in American society commanded substantial organizational attention in the GI Forum's initial years. As Allsup correctly notes,

> While many problems and issues required and received attention, the most immediate focus of the national organization became the critical needs of domestic farm workers . . . and the attendant issues of . . . *bracero* or Mexican contract worker and . . . the . . . illegal alien. The inherent and traditional Southwest relationship of cheap labor and large-scale agriculture had a detrimental effect, especially on the Mexican-American farm laborer. The presence of the . . . *bracero* maintained and exacerbated this condition. Because the agribusiness sector engendered strong support from many government officials, the possibility of improving life standards of the migrant workers was not promising. In addition, the complexities of the economic and international facets of the farm labor issue made it a difficult matter to resolve.[15]

Forum leaders pursued an immigration program primarily designed to assist Mexican-American workers, including proposals to repatriate illegal laborers, increase border surveillance, strictly enforce *bracero* contract requirements and restrictions, and discontinue the *bracero* program upon termination of its extension date in Congress— originally 1954 under Public Law 78.

In October 1953, the Forum and the American Federation of Labor (AFL) co-published an influential report outlining the problems attributable to undocumented labor. Titled *What Price Wetbacks?* and written by Ed Idar, Jr., with A. C. McLellan, the report studied such immigration-related problems as ineffective law enforcement, inadequacies in existing border statutes, and negative influences on American wage-earners, retail businesses, and health standards throughout the border region.[16] The study echoed previous Forum criticism of state and federal failure to enforce immigration, labor, and other laws along the border, and it called for increased border surveillance. When "Operation Wetback" went into effect, then, the Forum expressed approval of the program's endeavor to achieve these ends. On the other hand, it did not condone the INS's heavy-handed tactics, and Forum protests were substantial where *mexicanos* were needlessly harassed by Immigration Service police.

Balancing the competing interests of stricter immigration law enforcement with expanded rights for *mexicanos* was a complex, sometimes painful undertaking for the GI Forum. But the organization's own internal contradictions, as much as the complexities of government immigration policy, compelled it to try. Rank and file Forum members were highly patriotic and essentially conservative. They believed for the most part that U. S. jobs should be reserved for American citizens. Conversely, as Mexican Americans with strong familial, linguistic, and cultural ties to Mexico, Forumeers felt a special kinship to and responsibility for *bracero* and other Mexican workers in the United States. Inevitably, these sentiments were difficult to reconcile.

What helped most to keep Forum principals balanced in this dichotomy of interests was their early recognition that the immigration problem was not created by undocumented Mexican workers, but by large agricultural and industrial interests. Forum leaders were highly critical of depressed wages and poor working conditions. Furthermore, they frequently challenged business claims that American workers were unavailable or unwilling to do the work needed. Hector García, Vicente Ximenes, and others conducted surveys documenting numerous areas where adequate American workers could be found willing but unable to work in labor markets they had been priced out of by depressed wages resulting from the influx of exploited Mexican laborers.

These surveys, however, convinced Forum leaders that despite illegal immigrants' relative innocence and undeniable need for employment, their continued presence was creating a business- and state-legitimated hardship. By demanding the Bracero Program's discontinuation and strict enforcement of immigration laws, Forum leaders sought to undermine business rationales and justifications for further Mexican labor exploitation and denial of employment to American workers. Though progressively effective in securing support from important Democrats such as Hubert Humphrey, Paul Douglas, and Herbert Lehman, early Forum efforts to inspire immigration reform were overwhelmed by big business interests and their political allies. The Bracero Program was perennially reauthorized and manipulated as needed to meet private sector objectives for nearly fifteen years following the Forum's arrival on the scene in 1948; and when the program was finally discontinued in 1964, extensive mechanization in farming and production had substantially reduced the number of jobs available to be filled by domestic workers.[17] In the interim of continued *mexicano* exploitation and struggle, however, GI Forum efforts were ongoing and significant.

In large part these efforts involved attempts to increase public awareness of the growing use of undocumented Mexican labor in the American economy and the injustices this created throughout the southwestern and midwestern United States. Following the release of *What Price Wetbacks?*, the Forum produced important, new worker-related study findings, which outlined the lack of participation by Hispanic farm workers in the exchange of government benefits and entitlements. Released in a January 1956 Forum news bulletin, these findings showed that Mexican-American farm workers were frequently eligible for welfare assistance but, due to a combination of their apprehension towards official processes and the indifference of public administrators, few of these workers benefited.[18] Similar circumstances applied to migrant workers where social security and educational benefits were concerned. Furthermore, these workers rarely served on juries or voted. Thus disenfranchised from America's fundamental judicial and electoral processes, Mexican-American farm workers lacked the necessary political and legal impetus to enforce fair employment practice acts or anti-discrimination laws. The results were predictable: starvation wages, back-breaking work, poor medical attention, minimal education, and substandard housing.

Underlying these hardships were fundamental, structural impediments to the *mexicano* pursuit of justice and equal opportunity. Mexican Americans, whether on farms or in the cities, were frequently subjected to discrimination and exclusion in schools, housing, restaurants, hospitals, and other establishments. As a class, they were typically excluded from serving on public boards, commissions, and juries. Of course, *mexicanos* who were not U. S. citizens could not legally vote, but even those who *were* citizens were impeded by intimidation and poll taxation. The inequity was pervasive. GI Forum leaders and members did not stand by idly offering studies and statements alone. They confronted official denials of Mexican-American civil rights through direct action.

In Texas, the Forum took a leading role in prosecuting police brutality cases. In Mercedes, for example, it successfully secured the resignation of officer Darrill Holmes on June 20, 1953. Holmes had severely intimidated grocer George Saenz and his wife during an exchange at the Saenz's neighborhood store. As a result of the abuse, Saenz had to be medically treated for a serious nervous disorder. Later that same year, Forum lawyers successfully handled the case of Ernest García. On September 16, García was shot in the chest by Fort Worth police officer Vernon Johnson. The shooting followed a verbal altercation between Johnson and García family members, who had asked the officer to show a seizure warrant prior to entering their home. Forum legal efforts in the case helped to secure an aggravated assault charge against Johnson.

To challenge the notion that Mexican Americans could be legally barred from mainstream civic affairs, Forum leaders pursued numerous precedent-setting endeavors. Between 1951 and 1954, for example, Forum attorneys undertook a case involving the exclusion of Mexican Americans on Texas juries that ultimately took them to the U. S. Supreme Court. Jackson County farm worker Pete Hernández had been tried and convicted of murder, and sentenced to life imprisonment under Texas state law. Forum attorneys appealed the decision, arguing that Hernández had been denied the right to a trial before a jury of his peers. No Mexican Americans had served on his jury, nor had any Mexican American or Hispanic person been sought or selected for jury duty in the county's previous twenty-five years of recording jurors; in fact, only Anglo members of the county had been empaneled. The Forum's arguments were heard before the State Court of Criminal Appeals, but the lower court decision was upheld.

Following the unsuccessful effort to reverse the trial court ruling, Gus García filed an application to be heard before the U. S. Supreme Court. The Court agreed to hear the case, and GI Forum and LULAC members shared court processing fees and attorneys expenses. On January 11, 1954, the Forum's team of attorneys, comprised of Gus García, Carlos Cadena, James De Anda, Cris Alderete, John Herrera, and Maury Maverick, Jr., presented their arguments to the Warren Court.

Carlos Cadena initiated arguments for *Pete Hernández, Petitioner v. State of Texas*, observing that (1) Hernández had been convicted by a court and a county wherein no persons of Mexican or Latin American descent served as jurors or jury commissioners, or had even been called for jury service in the preceding twenty-five years; (2) the Hispanic persons denied these positions were qualified to serve; and (3) discrimination and segregation were common practices in Jackson County, where Mexican Americans were treated as a "race, class or group apart from all other persons."[19] Gus García delivered the Forum's primary contentions, acknowledging that while the Texas jury selection system was fair on its face and capable of nondiscriminatory use, those who oversaw its implementation *did* discriminate owing to their exclusion of otherwise eligible individuals solely on the basis of ethnicity. García then asserted that such jury exclusion violated constitutional prohibition of group or class discrimination under the Fourteenth Amendment.

Reflecting the absurdity of governmental racial policy during this period, Texas attorneys responded in the first instance by arguing that because Mexican Americans were legally considered white, they could not be underrepresented as jurors in Jackson County under prevailing circumstances. Then they argued that the historical absence of Spanish surnames on Jackson County jury rolls did not itself *prove* systematic exclusion. The state surmised that the lack of Hispanic representation on Jackson County juries was merely a coincidence.

On May 3, 1954—twelve days before the Court's historic ruling in *Brown v. Board of Education*—Chief Justice Earl Warren responded to these arguments. Addressing his opinion to the State of Texas' contention that coincidence explained the lack of Mexican Americans on juries, Warren stated:

> Circumstances or chance may well decide that no persons in a certain class will serve on a particular jury or during some particular period. But it taxes our credibility to say that mere chance resulted in there being no members of this class among the over six thousand jurors called in the past twenty-five years. The result bespeaks discrimination, whether or not it was a conscious decision on the part of any individual commissioner.

Finding unanimously for Hernández, the court reversed the Texas court rulings.

Hernández constituted the first resounding concurrence from the nation's highest court that Mexican Americans were indeed being treated as a class apart from the mainstream community, and that this denied them equal treatment under the law in violation of constitutional tenets. The *Hernández* decision secured U. S. constitutional landmark status on behalf of Mexican Americans, a critical and needed new tool in the evolving movement to expand rights and opportunities in America.

The Forum's role in helping to take the case successfully to the nation's highest court no doubt strengthened its standing to pursue other important and needed civil rights victories. In New Mexico, for example, in 1955, the Forum was able to secure through the state legislature passage of an anti-discrimination law similar to versions the GI Forum had proposed unsuccessfully there and in Texas in 1951 and 1953. The 1951 bill had died in the Texas house after passage in the state senate. Its provisions called for an end to monetary qualifications for voting in elections, neighborhood clauses in real estate contracts, and segregation in public places and private establishments serving the public. The 1953 New Mexico bill went beyond this, specifying monetary fines, prison terms, and license revocations for violations of the law's provisions. That bill was killed by a tie vote in the lower house of the legislature.

But following the Supreme Court's *Hernández* decision, the Forum took the lead in resurrecting anti-discrimination legislation in New Mexico. Under the leadership of Vicente Ximenes and Louis Téllez, support for a new bill was secured from LULAC, the National Association for the Advancement of Colored People (NAACP), the American Federation of Labor (AFL), and New Mexico Catholic hierarchy. During the 1955 legislative session, a version of the bill was passed, although without the strength of the sanctions endorsed by the Forum. Still, the final legislation did contain unprecedented provisions for court action and contempt proceedings for civil rights violators and continuous offenders, which the Forum had championed and helped to develop.

The law's passage was clearly a victory for the Forum, but it was not without its violators. In August 1956, it was discovered that the constitution of the New Mexico Brotherhood of Locomotive Firemen and Enginemen contained a blatantly discriminatory passage related to the acceptance of Brotherhood members:

> [Members] shall be white, born of good moral character, sober and industrious, no less than sixteen years of age, and be able to read and write the English language and understand our constitution. Mexicans or those of Spanish extraction are not eligible. [20]

Upon learning of the passage, New Mexico Forumeers immediately filed a complaint with the New Mexico Fair Employment Practices Commission and demanded an investigation. The Brotherhood denied any discrimination, but refused to supply authorities with an official copy of its constitution pending the decision of an Ohio court case pertaining to the same issue. The Forum heightened its local demands for punitive action against the Brotherhood and pursued federal intervention through the assistance of U. S. Senators Dennis Chávez (D-NM) and Ralph Yarborough (D-TX), both of whom agreed to support an investigation by a presidential committee on government contracts. As a result of these and other Forum-inspired pressures, the Brotherhood agreed in January, 1958, to delete the exclusionary reference to Hispanic persons.[21]

Despite the Forum's relative successes in promoting—and frequently in applying—anti-discrimination laws and sanctions in states such as New Mexico, Forum leaders understood that legislation of this type would not by itself end discrimination against Mexican Americans and others. The Forum alone could never put an end to this, but the organization could strive to make known discrimination and civil rights violations to Americans of all persuasions. It could appeal firmly to the common interests of all people to play their part in ending such injustices. It could help to inspire and direct community and civic action to denounce racial bigotry and intolerance. This is what the Forum did so well. A 1957 incident in Colorado helps to illustrate this point.

In early February of that year, the Daughters of the American Revolution (DAR) sponsored a Lincoln Day celebration at the Colorado Industrial School for Boys, a state correctional institute for young men assigned there by juvenile and county authorities. Many of

the school's boys were Mexican-American youths, and several participated in flag-carrying and marching ceremonies at the DAR
celebration. During the program, the local DAR chairwoman voiced
concern over the large number of "Mexicans" assigned to these tasks.
"They are Mexican boys, not American boys," she was heard to com-
plain. Later the DAR officer commented that she would not have
permitted a Mexican to carry the American flag at such a gathering.

When news of the incident spread to members of the Colorado GI
Forum, state chairman Art Tafoya issued a formal protest to both
Colorado DAR officials and Denver newspapers. Contacted by
reporters to confirm her statements at the Lincoln Day celebration, the
woman responded, "I wouldn't want a Mexican to carry Old Glory,
would you?" The Forum's national office instructed all state and local
chapters to respond by writing not only DAR officials, but also their
congressmen and senators. Not surprisingly, the situation provoked an
energetic response from across the nation.

In response, Governor Stephen L. R. McNichols ordered an immediate suspension of DAR activities in Colorado, pending a review of
the organization's official attitudes. U. S. Senator Dennis Chávez, a
strong Forum ally on many issues, also responded by sending a
staunchly written reprimand to Colorado DAR officials, which read in
part: "576 'Mexicans' were among those carrying the American flag at
Bataan in World War II; what makes you think they can't carry it just
as proudly in Colorado?"

The DAR's national president soon formally repudiated the local
Colorado officer's statements on behalf of the entire organization. She
also extended an invitation to Forum national officials to join her in a
goodwill exchange of large American flags. Shortly thereafter, DAR
officials joined Forum leaders at the Forum's national headquarters in
Albuquerque to follow through. During the highly publicized ceremony, DAR leaders publicly praised the Forum's work and the
achievements of American soldiers of Mexican descent.[22]

Following the DAR's action, Governor McNichols ended the
moratorium on DAR activity in Colorado and official pressure from the
GI Forum was halted. But the DAR had been badly embarrassed by the
incident, and, more importantly, others had duly observed the Forum's

power of public appeal and its preparedness to use that power in response to discriminatory statements and practices.

In south Texas, Forum appeals to eradicate prejudice and discrimination were met with increasing retaliation by powerful racist elements. Forum efforts there were thus less evidently successful, but no less hard-fought. In 1957, Hector García was informed by an organization of Mexican-American laborers that numerous violations of *mexicano* labor and civil rights were occurring at the Mathis, Texas, agricultural concern of F. H. Vahlsing, Inc. After interviewing company employees at the group's request, the doctor contacted state officials and the Mexican consulate in Corpus Christi to inform them of violations he had documented at Vahlsing, involving both Mexican and Mexican-American workers. The Forum's intervention resulted in a U. S. Department of Labor investigation. The investigation determined that Vahlsing had failed to advertise available jobs for domestic laborers in accordance with the *bracero* agreement and had used light-weighted scales to cheat *bracero* laborers of their legal wages. The Forum's complaint and the Labor Department's subsequent findings forced Vahlsing to reimburse *bracero* workers for a total of $3,509.27 in wages withheld.

Predictably, the Anglo community of Mathis did not respond favorably to the Forum's involvement in the matter. Already García and other Forumeers had commenced legal action against discriminatory school officials and policies in Mathis. Following the Vahlsing incident, one group of Mathis citizens decided they had had enough of Hector García and the GI Forum. Informed that Dr. García would be attending an official Forum meeting in Mathis, the group organized a vigilante committee to wait outside the meeting hall with sticks and clubs for the purpose of "welcoming" the Forum's founder. The group was surprised when the "Dr. García" in question turned out to be a woman: Dr. Clotilde García, Hector García's sister (also a physician). She had been scheduled to speak at a GI Forum women's gathering.

Some time after this occurrence, one Mathis resident confronted Hector García about the Forum's activities, stating:

> . . . You're a doctor, an educated man. And you're light-skinned, almost like us. You don't have to involve yourself in these controversies. You could have 'most anything you want probably. But you

want to cause all these problems because you expect us to treat all
your people equal, let 'em in our schools, in our clubs, no matter how
dark some of 'em may be. We just can't have that . . . If we educate
these people, or send some of these Mexicans back across the border,
well, who'll pick our cotton?

At least in later years Forum and other community efforts would
be strengthened by the establishment of legal and administrative protections, but during the 1950s the Forum was frequently on its own in
its battles. Initially, Forum leaders envisioned attacking inequities
mainly through Mexican-American involvement in local education and
civic affairs. Soon, in addition to this, however, they recognized the
need for substantially greater influence in the political arena. Only
through such influence would Mexican Americans ever secure
accountability in government and society. This notion compelled
expanding Forum efforts to confront the violation of civil rights, to gain
the support of mainstream politicians, to secure the appointment of
Mexican Americans to juries and important public boards and commissions, and then to promote the election of Mexican Americans to
positions of political influence. Each of these objectives was defined as
an essential element of the Forum's program, but the entire concept
was finally tied to one critical variable: voting.

In Texas, Mexican-American voting rights were restricted in part
by the introduction of the poll tax. The poll tax required every voting
citizen of the state to pay a "minimal" $1.75 per year to participate in
statewide, regional, and local elections. Payment of the tax supposedly
demonstrated the vested interest each good citizen of the state held in
supporting the electoral process. But the required fee was highly pro-
hibitive for Mexican Americans and other low-income minorities. In
1960, the per capita *yearly* income of Mexican Americans was
$968.00, or approximately $19 per week. Seen from this perspective
$1.75 is somewhat less minimal than Texas voting authorities appar-
ently assumed.

Along with LULAC, the Forum supported campaigns to promote
Mexican-American voter participation and "pay your poll tax" drives.
Complementing these activities were continuous Forum efforts to eliminate the poll tax altogether. The latter efforts, however, were generally
fruitless. Some Texas politicians dared to extend proposals to eliminate

the poll tax but never with favorable results. Year after year, Forum conventions passed resolutions denouncing poll taxation and supporting efforts aimed at its repeal, but the tax was an embedded relic of Texas' two-tiered society. Forum leaders were not unaware of this.[23] As a result, the Forum pushed more and more strongly for reform through that very mechanism of change which the state sought to deny Mexican-American citizens—the power of votes. Efforts to increase Mexican-American voter participation spread to Forum chapters around the country during the 1950s, supported by the familiar array of social activities (dances, sales, rallies, etc.). But these efforts were concentrated in south Texas, where the poll tax and Anglo dominance created the greatest electoral inequities for *mexicanos.*

A 1955-1956 poll-tax drive in the Rio Grande Valley led to the organization of the Rio Grande Democratic Club, a coalition intended to simplify and coordinate the efforts of area groups working to register Mexican-American voters. Robert P. Sánchez, a McAllen attorney and Forumeer, headed the club. The GI Forum's efforts in the drive were augmented by LULAC, the AFL-CIO, the Texas Brotherhood of Railroad Workers, and U. S. Senator Dennis Chávez of New Mexico. In the end, the drive significantly altered voting imbalances in the counties of Hidalgo, Cameron, and Willacy. Prior to the Valley-wide drive, only 43 percent of these counties' combined electorates were Mexican-American, despite the fact that they made up more than 75 percent of the region's population. By the end of the drive, Mexican-Americans held a 53 percent share of the Valley's voting population.[24] It marked the first time in history that the Mexican-American population of that area constituted a voting majority.

Anglo-owned newspapers in Harlingen, McAllen, and Brownsville were fiercely critical of the poll-tax drive, citing the Forum's involvement and the AFL-CIO's support as evidence of a conspiracy to take over the Valley.[25] Many Anglo Texans reacted in terms typical of the times by labeling the Forum's efforts "communist-inspired." Senator Chávez, who spoke at several of the rallies, was described as a traitor to the American farmer, and editorials accused the drive's supporters of promoting racial and class conflict.[26] These reactions inspired further denunciations of the drive. Governor Allan Shivers called for an investigation of the Rio Grande Democratic Club, alleging that misused union and public funds might have assisted the drive. The state attorney general, however, later cleared the Forum of any wrongdoing.

During the Christmas season coinciding with the poll tax drive, McAllen retailers refused to contribute to the town's perennially business-supported Forum benefit for underprivileged children. And the following Veteran's Day, American Legion, Veterans of Foreign Wars, and National Guardsmen chapters refused to march with Forum chapters in commemorative parades and festivities, on the grounds that the Forum was not a veterans organization but rather a political faction. In a published response, Forumeer Ed Idar Jr. wrote:

> We have come to a sad day in Texas democracy when an organization of veterans cannot join in efforts to promote of all things the sale of poll taxes to citizens in an area where the record shows that the majority of citizens never have qualified themselves to vote . . . Members of the GI Forum paid for the right to participate in poll tax drives with the blood, the guts and the lives of their comrades left overseas . . . and only a warped and twisted logic can come out with the principle that National Guardsmen who are subject to pay the same price in the future must not march shoulder to shoulder with men who already have done so on a day set aside to commemorate the sacrifices that America's fighting men of all backgrounds made to make such commemoration possible.[27]

Such reactions were saddening, but by no means surprising. These were reactions of fear and anxiety that the Anglo-dominated socioeconomic and political order was being shaken. According to Allsup, Anglo concern and outrage met Forum efforts to mobilize new Valley voters owing to

> . . . fear that the traditional feudal agricultural empire of the Rio Grande was being threatened. Voter strength translated into political power could affect the grower dominated 25¢ per hour labor system which depended on *mojados* (illegal workers) and *braceros* (contract workers) from Mexico. The very idea that the five percent of the population which had historically controlled the remaining 95 percent *mexicanos* might actually have to share political power was intolerable.

So too, though, was it intolerable for GI Forum members to conceive of another hundred years of subjugation. The restrictive poll tax remained in place after 1955-1956, but the Forum's increasingly successful voter registration efforts were continued. In the presidential election of 1960 the significance of the Mexican-American vote would be felt in an unprecedented way.

During 1959-1960, Democratic politicians harnessed the Mexican-American vote to help propel John F. Kennedy into the White House through the establishment of "Viva Kennedy" clubs, which were organized by Carlos McCormick of Arizona (later a charter member of the Forum's Washington, D. C. chapter). Throughout the Southwest and Midwest, "Viva Kennedy" clubs brought the Kennedy appeal to the Mexican-American community. According to National Council of La Raza President Raúl Yzaguirre, who participated extensively in GI Forum youth leadership activities during these years in Texas, Kennedy captured the imagination of Hispanics through his youth, his projected sensitivity to the needs of the underprivileged, and his immigrant Catholic background.[28] Kennedy's strong following among Mexican-American voters paid welcome dividends in 1960. Despite the presence of Lyndon Johnson on the presidential ticket, the senator from Massachusetts could not have won Texas without that state's overwhelmingly Democratic Mexican-American vote. Kennedy defeated Richard Nixon by the smallest voting margin in modern presidential election history.

Kennedy's presidency and the Mexican-American contribution to his election raised *mexicano* political sights to new levels. Effective new organizations grew out of the "Viva Kennedy" experience: MAPA (Mexican American Political Association) in California, and PASSO (Political Association of Spanish-Speaking Organizations) in Texas. And in 1961 and 1962, respectively, Henry B. González of San Antonio and Edward Roybal of Los Angeles were elected to the U. S. Congress. With all this a new Mexican-American political consciousness was born. Now Mexican Americans not only sought to demand change from the grassroots, outside the political process, they also expected to influence change as participants within the political process itself.

In many respects Kennedy's presidency left Mexican-American expectations largely unfulfilled, yet his unprecedented recognition of America's race problems and his assassination served ultimately to legitimate and bolster the civil-rights movements of the 1960s and 1970s. These years would see the development of new laws and programs aimed at bringing justice and equal opportunity to American minorities of all backgrounds. They would see the abolition of the Bracero Program and the poll tax. For Mexican Americans in particular, the results would not always be fully satisfactory, nor would the problems of greatest concern be fully addressed. But where there were improvements, they would be real and significant; and they would make the American dream a more tangible concept for previously unimagined numbers of Hispanic people. To all of this, the GI Forum's contributions were great.

Chapter 5

The Kennedy and Johnson Years

In recounting his years spent working for John F. Kennedy, Pierre Salinger alludes to the possibility that Kennedy began running for president as early as 1956, following his unsuccessful bid for the vice-presidential nomination at the Democratic National Convention.[1] Kennedy's early inroads into the Hispanic voting population would indicate as much. The future president's initial exposure to the plight of the *mexicano* came in his first term in the U. S. Senate. At that time, Kennedy participated extensively in hearings on the Bracero Program. In 1957, he sponsored an important immigrant-families reunification bill, which he led to passage in the senate with the Forum's support.[2] Kennedy's second senatorial term saw the appointment of Carlos McCormick (a Forumeer from Arizona) to the Kennedy staff in Washington, D. C. It was McCormick who masterminded the "Viva Kennedy" concept and who set its structure in place well in advance of the 1960 presidential election.

The establishment of the "Viva Kennedy" network played an important role in enhancing the influence of individual Forumeers in the presidential election outcome; for, while the Forum was endlessly assailed by its critics as a political machine, and while it would be difficult to argue that the Forum was not a political group, in fact, the GI Forum constitution precluded organizational officers and members from endorsing or campaigning on behalf of partisan political candidates, except outside of their formal affiliation with the group as individuals.[3] "Viva Kennedy" clubs gave Forumeers the organizational mechanism they needed to play a direct role in the Democratic presidential campaign without violating the GI Forum's institutional integrity. Thus many leaders of the Forum's 150 local chapters were prominent during the Kennedy campaign in organizing and leading such clubs.

In 1959, Kennedy actively began to court Mexican-American voters. Among other gestures, he sent a particularly warm message of congratulations to the national GI Forum convention that year in Los Angeles. The following June, the senator officially became a member of the Forum, which he called "a splendid organization of Spanish-speaking ex-servicemen."[4] The broadening of Kennedy's relationship with national Hispanic leaders continued as the candidate and his brother and campaign manager, Robert, engaged Hector García and others in frank discussions regarding the Democrats' civil rights plank. In the process, the Kennedys committed to a formidable list of civil-rights pledges; these included enforcement of school desegregation mandates established by the Supreme Court, support of equal employment opportunity and fair housing legislation, and federal protections for minority voters and migrant laborers.[5]

After Kennedy edged out Richard Nixon by the narrowest margin in modern presidential election history, he personally thanked Hector García and other Hispanic Americans for delivering critical votes that helped to ensure his victory.[6] In Illinois, a changeover of only 9,000 votes would have put Nixon in the White House. In Texas, 50,000 votes would have made the difference. Both states carried strong "Viva Kennedy" organizations. Mexican-Americans everywhere rejoiced in the Kennedy victory and their role in making it a possibility.[7] Moreover, they enthusiastically looked forward to playing a direct role in helping to formulate and implement Kennedy administration policy.

Initially, the new administration's response was encouraging. Ambassadorial posts were immediately offered to Hector García and Henry B. Gonzáles. However, both declined appointment due to other commitments. Soon, thereafter, García was appointed by Kennedy to negotiate a mutual defense and aid agreement with the Federation of West Indies Islands, and George I. Sánchez, the noted educator and

LULAC leader, was appointed to the influential Citizens Committee on New Frontier Policy in the Americas.[8]

But the notion of *mexicano* political influence in the Kennedy administration was quickly put to question. Small legislative victories for migrant workers and the discontinuation of the Bracero Program during Kennedy's thousand days were offset in the minds of Mexican-American leaders by his failure to push for more enduring civil rights legislation, by his relative dearth of Mexican-American appointments to high-level administration posts, and by the failure of his brother's Justice Department to more actively challenge violations of *mexicano* civil rights. When the president did finally turn to civil rights and to race issues in the last year of his life, he did so by defining the problems as if they pertained only to conflicts between whites and black Americans, further prolonging the Mexican American's forgotten status.

Still, Kennedy's presidency marked a turning point for America's Hispanic population. JFK's accessibility to Hispanic leaders was unprecedented, and his concomitant appeal to the Hispanic people was an important factor in enhancing the strength and direction of their political activity. Furthermore, his belated but inspiring attention to black civil rights helped to redefine the nation's domestic agenda. The landmark Civil Rights Act of 1964, which was basically Kennedy's proposal, would lay a foundation for social reform that would inspire major institutional change, and with this new vistas and opportunities not only for long-denied black Americans, but also for Latinos and other historically disadvantaged American groups.

When Robert Kennedy addressed the GI Forum national convention at Chicago in July, 1963, therefore, emphasis was placed not on the disappointments of President Kennedy's first term but rather on the hopes and promises for the future. With a second term, it was asserted, a stronger and even more committed President Kennedy would boldly lead the struggle for justice and equal opportunity for Hispanic and other minority Americans. Kennedy's second term never came, but his legacy heightened the opportunity for Lyndon Johnson to forge profound social change on behalf of America's disadvantaged. Johnson seized the opportunity to undertake the building of a "Great Society."

Doris Kearns Goodwin, a White House Fellow during the Johnson presidency and author of the biography *Lyndon Johnson and the American Dream*, suggests that LBJ's mammoth Great Society program was the product both of his personal search for greatness and a unique convergence of historical events.[9] The shock of Kennedy's assassination, the civil-rights movement, an emerging awareness of the extent of poverty in what for a few had become an affluent society— all of these factors combined to focus American public energies and perceptions on domestic problems. According to Kearns Goodwin,

> the Great Society was a response to—indeed part of—gradually emerging currents in American awareness . . . the sense that . . . the means we had devised to create wealth had consequences that were beginning to threaten and degrade humanity. Along with the civil rights and peace movements came consumerism, environmentalism and women's liberation, all protests against the system, not just for its economic deficiencies, but at its constriction of possibilities for human fulfillment.

At bottom, then, the Great Society found its roots in those aspects of the American dream which proposed that all Americans should benefit equally from the system; but, its aims transcended mere material attainment and sought, through a redistribution of wealth and resources, to ensure human fulfillment for the diversity of society's groups and individuals. Thus, the Great Society included not only massive increases in direct-relief efforts to assist the needy (e.g., Medicare-Medicaid, Aid to Families with Dependent Children, etc.), but also an ambitious program embodied in Johnson's "War on Poverty," with its correlating endeavors in education, job and skills training, neighborhood development, and community relations. The Great Society drew heavily from Franklin Roosevelt's New Deal in its breadth, and from John Kennedy's New Frontier in its idealistic appeal to progressives, minorities, and the young. But Lyndon Johnson's personality and ambition saw to it that his contribution to American society *vis-a-vis* Roosevelt's and Kennedy's would even more broadly touch the lives of American citizens, particularly the disadvantaged. The Great Society embellished the New Deal and the New Frontier with essential elements of Johnson's own personality, and undertook to achieve unprecedented levels of social reform that would distinctly conclude the work that Roosevelt and Kennedy had only begun.

From the outset, civil rights supporters were skeptical of Johnson. He was seen as a southern Democrat at a time when southern Democrats were politically conservative. But, gradually, as he demonstrated his commitment to carrying out—and expanding on—the civil-rights program inherited from Kennedy, civil-rights leaders began to applaud LBJ's efforts.

GI Forum leaders held more than just a tentative faith in Lyndon Johnson, borne out of a relationship dating back to the Felix Longoria incident at Three Rivers in 1948. Johnson's show of compassion and concern towards *mexicano* people had been overwhelming then as he personally arranged Longoria's burial at Arlington National Cemetery with full military honors (an action that longtime Johnson associate D. B. Hardeman would later suggest could only have hurt Johnson politically in Texas, but which he pursued because "what the people in Three Rivers did outraged him").[10]

After the Longoria affair, Johnson had further assisted Forum efforts in quiet but important ways. He had helped the Forum, for example, to desegregate Army medical facilities in south Texas. Prior to Johnson's intervention, these facilities practiced ward segregation, placing whites in more endowed treatment areas, while minority patients were directed to lesser quarters. Johnson had also helped to advance Forum efforts to contest discriminatory hiring and employment practices at U. S. postal facilities in the region. In Corpus Christi, for example, the local post office's nine service windows had never been staffed by Mexican-American workers. Johnson supported a special investigation of these practices which resulted in needed changes.

Forum relations with Johnson cooled during the 1950s, as his national prominence expanded. Johnson frequently associated with southern Democrats; and when he ascended to lead the senate majority, his efforts to advance civil rights became almost negligible.[11] But the JFK/LBJ presidential ticket brought Johnson and many influential Forumeers closer together again. These old ties were further reinforced through Johnson's relatively unproductive vice-presidency, which, despite diminished influence, enabled Johnson to advance important civil rights proposals as chairman of the President's Committee on Equal Opportunity. In that capacity, Johnson frequently called upon the advice and expertise of Hector García and other GI Forum leaders.

Based on this long history with Johnson, GI Forum principals fully expected to be more centrally involved in presidential policymaking under LBJ than they had been during the Kennedy administration. Indeed, Forum and other Mexican-American community leaders would figure prominently during Johnson's years as president, though sometimes in ways that would not comport with the president's agenda.

The passage of the Voting Rights Act of 1965 marked Johnson's initial investment in the Great Society. His Justice Department had been instructed to draft legislation following mounting pressure from Hector García and other Mexican Americans in Texas regarding the injustice of poll taxation. At the beginning of 1965, highly publicized confrontations over black voting rights in Alabama and other states accelerated the administration's resolve to pass a voting rights bill in the first congressional session of Johnson's elected presidency. The decision was a bold one to sustain in the wake of intense racial tensions throughout the South and the Southwest, and it convinced many Johnson critics that in fact the president was more than just rhetorically committed to bringing about a "Great Society."

For Mexican Americans and other Hispanic people, the president's introduction of the Voting Rights Act before a joint session of Congress was a bittersweet moment. Johnson's legislation did not finally carry provisions covering Hispanics as beneficiaries. The omission was especially troubling to Forum and other Mexican-American leaders, who had expected more of Johnson, given his direct knowledge of voting irregularities in Texas and other states. It would take much more hard work and another decade for Mexican-American leaders to gain coverage of Hispanic voters, in the Act's 1975 extension, to remedy this shortcoming in Johnson's proposal.[12] On the other hand, LBJ's emotional, nationally televised remarks on the Voting Rights Act marked the first time an American president had placed America's race problems outside the parameters of merely black/white relations. In fact, Johnson's remarks bore special significance for their relevance to Mexican Americans across the United States.

In his speech, Johnson explained to Congress and the nation that his convictions on the issue of voting rights were rooted in his experience as a young teacher of Mexican-American children in the south Texas town of Cotulla.

> My students were poor, and they often came to class without breakfast, hungry. They knew even in their youth the pain of injustice. They never understood why people disliked them, but they knew it was so, because I saw it in their eyes. I often walked home late in the afternoon, after the classes were finished, wishing there was more I could do . . .
>
> Somehow you never forget what poverty and hatred can do when you see its scars on the hopeful face of a young child. I never thought then, in 1928, that I would be standing here in 1965. It never occurred to me in my fondest dreams that I might have the chance to help the sons and daughters of those students and to help people like them all over the country. But now I do have that chance, and I'll let you in on a secret, I mean to use it.

The rapid acceleration of Johnson's War on Poverty and the president's own actions in the months following these remarks suggest that LBJ sincerely meant to use his power and position to bring about meaningful change for *mexicanos*. In a series of appointments the president named Hector García, Louis Téllez, Larry Ramírez, and Rodolfo "Corky" Gonzáles (all Forumeers) to a national committee to oversee the federal Community Relations Service. Thereafter, Ramírez and Gonzáles were appointed to important regional posts at War on Poverty agencies in Kansas City and Denver respectively. Ed Terrones, the Forum's national vice-chairman, was appointed to a high-ranking position under the office of the postmaster general. And Vicente Ximenes was named to a central position under Sergeant Shriver at the nerve center of the Johnson program: the Office of Economic Opportunity (OEO). Other Mexican Americans were recruited into appointed positions in the Departments of Health, Education, and Welfare; Labor; and Justice.[13] Rural assistance programs were expanded to include *mexicano* federal employees not only in Washington but at the local and regional offices where Great Society programs operated.

These actions were highly encouraging. Never before had the Mexican-American community experienced such proximity to the American presidency. The Great Society and its budding programs seemed to coincide greatly with the priorities of the Hispanics, and dis-advantaged persons everywhere. Particularly among disaffected minorities, the poor, youths, progressives, and intellectuals, the dynam-ic initially at work in the Great Society promoted new faith and far-reaching trust in Lyndon Johnson, its chief orchestrator.

Alas, all this would change dramatically during the course of Johnson's presidency. During 1966-1968, a host of domestic and for-eign problems—some of Johnson's own making, others informed by more deep-rooted weaknesses in established American policy—would thrust American society into unprecedented turmoil. For Mexican Americans and others, as well, these years would mark a sea-change in the American experience, exacting from many their faith in American ideals and from most their trust in Lyndon Johnson.

Aside from Hector García, who wielded a uniquely influential rela-tionship with LBJ, the most persuasive representative of Hispanic concerns during the Johnson administration was Vicente Ximenes. Johnson's landslide victory in 1964 ensured Ximenes an important spot at the newly created Office of Economic Opportunity, out of which were being built the institutions that would provide artillery for Johnson's War on Poverty—Job Corps, Model Cities, Community Services, VISTA, *et al.* Early on, Ximenes sensed shortcomings in the organizational structures and designs of these programs, which fore-shadowed inevitable criticisms of Johnson and his notion of the Great Society.

To begin with, the programs were devoid of meaningful minority representation, especially in the decision-making stages of policy for-mulation. Minority appointments offered only scattered opportunities for those closest to the nation's inequities to *implement* program guide-lines, but minorities themselves had nothing whatsoever to do with defining these guidelines. Predictably, the guidelines failed to compre-hend community realities. In too many areas, federal bureaucrats oversaw the programs without much understanding of local needs.

Furthermore, to Ximenes, the programs were almost wholly lack-ing in recognition of the inequities suffered within Hispanic and other minority communities. For the overwhelming majority of Johnson administrators, poverty, unemployment, poor housing, ill health, and low educational attainment were identified as problems of southern and inner-city blacks and poor rural whites. Not a single Mexican-American population center appeared on any list Ximenes was shown of the hundreds of urban centers initially considered for Model Cities funding. A similar omission occurred in the initial establishment of Job Corps sites. Only Ximenes' fervent lobbying and the influence of Hector García secured San Marcos, Texas, on the final Job Corps centers roster.

Mexican-American leaders and activists became increasingly vocal about the War on Poverty's exclusions. Complaints began to reach Washington regarding the insensitivity of various federal programs towards the Hispanic, the still relative underrepresentation of Hispanic federal administrators, and Johnson's failure to carry out various commitments to Hispanic leaders. By early 1966, these criticisms reached a boiling point that would entirely change the composition of Hispanic-American politics in the months and years to come.

Underlying this growing dissatisfaction with Johnson's programs was a combination of historical forces and events that pushed Hispanic Americans into an unprecedented state of community awareness: the continuing black/white tenor of national policy debate constantly reminded Hispanic citizens of their forgotten status, the war in Vietnam saw Hispanic soldiers dying in numbers far above their proportion of the population, and the nationally publicized plight of César Chávez's farm labor movement dramatized the gross inequities experienced by migrant Hispanic workers. This succession of issues brought Mexican Americans and other Hispanics to the limits of their patience. They determined to make their voices heard in ways they had never been heard before.

Their effort was by no means monolithic. In the *mexicano* community there existed a split, largely though not wholly generational, between those opting for more vocal yet conventional protest within the mainstream, and those opting instead for a more militant protest. Militancy was most evident among the young, especially students, in the *barrios* and at colleges. Community elders generally sought a more accommodationist, though no less committed path. Throughout this process the American GI Forum remained at the forefront of Hispanic-American politics with organizational representatives in both camps of the community's emergent consciousness.

In California and Texas, GI Forumeers actively supported Chicano farm workers' efforts to secure state-based rights legislation, first through the National Farm Workers Association (NFWA) and later through its successor, the United Farm Workers (UFW). Although agribusiness and elected leaders conspired to limit or squelch these efforts, they were significant flashpoints in the development of Mexican-American political identity in the 1960s. According to Gómez-Quiñones,

> the dramatic organizational struggle of the UFW was a major cata-
> lyst in the development of Mexican politics. Support of the farm
> workers union was a major focus and inspiration for the political
> activism of the urban Mexican, the vast majority of whom had never
> been farm workers . . . From the mid-60s on, many Mexican activists
> from the center and left, and regardless of their political affiliation,
> concurred in supporting the farm workers cause.

Early in 1966, at its mid-year convention in Albuquerque, the Forum called upon its various state and local chapters to support the nearly year-long efforts of striking UFW grape pickers seeking higher wages and collective bargaining rights in Delano, California.[14] Significant Forum public-information and education activities followed in support. Shortly thereafter, U. S. Senator Harrison A. Williams of New Jersey led a congressional subcommittee to Delano to hear the strike representatives' grievances. After taking the testimony of the farm workers, the committee, which included New York Senator Robert F. Kennedy, promised to do something for California grape pickers. In April, a mass march was organized by the UFW to trek the 300 miles between Delano, in California's Central Valley, and the state capitol in Sacramento. More than fifty GI Forum state leaders participated in the march, representing chapters in Merced, Oakland, Richmond, San Jose, Santa Clara, Union City and Pittsburgh; and Forum lieutenants in Sacramento provided traffic and crowd control along the march route to the capitol, at UFW leader César Chávez's request.

The strikers intended to arrive in the capitol on Easter Sunday and present to Governor Edmund G. (Pat) Brown, Sr. and state legislators a formal petition that farm workers be granted legal rights and working conditions that would make their struggle on picket lines unnecessary

(Meister and Loftis 1977, 144). The marchers did not get what they wanted; Brown, fearful of alienating agricultural interests, refused to even meet with march leaders, deciding instead to spend the weekend with his family in Palm Springs at the home of Frank Sinatra (Meister and Loftis 1977, 145).

Brown's refusal to meet and his subsequent inattention to the marchers' objectives was not surprising to Chicano leaders, but it was disappointing and unacceptable. Early in his tenure, Brown's administration had reacted much more favorably to farm worker issues, certainly more than had any of its immediate predecessors. For example, Brown's director of employment, Al Tiebury, backed by a Brown majority on the California Supreme Court, had ruled that farms being picketed were involved in legitimate labor disputes, even though pickets might be organizers seeking union recognition rather than unionized employees demanding contracts. As Brown approached a reelection campaign in 1966 against charismatic conservative candidate Ronald Reagan, however, his position changed dramatically. He supported a grower-sponsored bill that would have blocked farm strikes and he allowed legislators to kill bills he had proposed (at the AFL-CIO's urging) for a state agricultural minimum wage and a farm labor commission.

A few days after the march on Sacramento, Brown visited San Jose, a GI Forum stronghold, to dedicate an industrial park. He was met by pickets, headed by GI Forum women's state chairwoman Anita Campos and members of the Forum's San Jose and Santa Clara women's groups. Campos confronted the governor and criticized him for not meeting pro-farm worker marchers on Easter Day. She implored him to introduce a measure for adequate farm worker protection in the forthcoming legislative session. "We want legislation *now*," Campos demanded. "We are tired of tomorrows!" Brown was visibly shaken by this unanticipated and unhappy encounter. When he regained his composure, he told television newsmen that he would do all he could for farm workers and that he hoped not to lose the political support of Mexican Americans. Unfortunately for Brown, his rift with the UFW, the Forum, and other key Mexican-American groups was already too severe to spare him from defeat in November.

In Texas, efforts to unionize farm laborers had been squelched historically by broken strikes, facilitated by Texas Rangers, local courts, and state right-to-work laws. In 1966, Texas farm workers' per capita annual income was a paltry $1,568; most workers earned less than $1 per hour. In June 1966, an UFW strike was called to gain a $1.75 per hour minimum farm wage. UFW members and friends marched from Rio Grande City to the state capitol in Austin, to take their case to Governor John Connally and other elected officials. In their trek through the Rio Grande Valley, marchers were greeted and joined along the way by GI Forum and LULAC members. Among the march leaders were Hector García and his sister Clotilde, who joined the group in Corpus Christi.

According to Rodolfo Acuña,

> On July 7, Al Ramírez, the mayor of Edinburgh, left his hospital bed to welcome the . . . marchers. The next day a thousand people gathered to hear mass at San Juan Catholic Shrine. Union people along the route warmly cheered the strikers. By July 30, they reached Corpus Christi. The small band wound its way along Highway 181, and in spite of heavy rain, over a thousand partisans waited for them in San Antonio, where a two-hour parade followed. Archbishop Lucey celebrated mass. The march to Austin continued.[15]

In Austin, ten thousand marchers converged on the capitol, where they were met by Governor Connally, State House Majority Speaker Ben Barnes, and Texas Attorney General Waggoner Carr. The strikers attempted to pressure Connally to call a special legislative session to pass a minimum-wage bill, but he refused to entertain the notion and informed march leaders that he did not plan to be in Austin on Labor Day.[16]

Ultimately, Texas UFW leaders were forced to retreat. But the Austin march, like the Sacramento march before it, had inspired its supporters, including significant numbers of GI Forum leaders and members, to redouble organized efforts to advance the Chicano political agenda in America.

In Washington, President Johnson announced the formation of a White House Conference, "To Fulfill These Rights." A cross-section of business, labor, and black civil-rights leaders was named to the Conference, which was "to help the American negro fulfill the rights which after the long time of injustice he is finally about to secure."[17] Mexican-American leaders were outraged by the president's retreat to black/white social policy. The action left increasing numbers in the Hispanic community without enthusiasm or incentive to further support Johnson's programs.

In Santa Clara, California and Albuquerque, New Mexico, GI Forum and other Hispanic leaders expressed their dissatisfaction with Johnson administration policies by staging walkouts at regional meetings of the Equal Employment Opportunity Commission (EEOC).[18] These actions were followed by the filing of a formal complaint with acting EEOC director John W. Macy, Jr. by an Ad Hoc Committee of Mexican-American Organizations. National GI Forum Chairman Augustine Flores submitted the complaint as chairman of the committee, citing the EEOC's deplorable underrepresentation of Hispanics. (Only two members of the Commission's 150 member staff were Hispanic.) Moreover, the complaint condemned the lack of Hispanic representation on the EEOC's Board of Commissioners, reminding Macy that the Hispanic population comprised the nation's second-largest minority group and had many qualified candidates.[19]

Rudy Ramos, the Forum's representative in the nation's capitol, threatened to file an injunction against the use of federal funds by the EEOC unless initiatives were forthcoming to address these grievances. Soon thereafter a national effort to demand a White House conference on Hispanic concerns began to take shape. Before a White House gathering on equal employment opportunity, Hector García presented a statement signed by Mexican-American community leaders calling for such a conference, as well as for the appointment of a Mexican-American presidential assistant to facilitate more fruitful communication between the Mexican-American community and the federal government. During a later press conference President Johnson responded that he felt he had done all he could to promote better understanding between Hispanics and his administration; however, he remarked, if a White House conference was necessary, one would be held.[20]

Following the press conference, Johnson assigned one of his chief aides, Joseph A. Califano, Jr., to search for qualified Mexican Americans to fill government posts and to organize a conference in

Texas for Mexican Americans comparable to the White House Conference on Civil Rights. On May 26, five of the community's top leaders, including Hector García and the Forum's National chairman, Augustine Flores, met with the president and Califano for dinner at the White House to discuss the conference. Other participating Mexican-American leaders included Bert Corona of MAPA, Roy Elizondo of PASSO, and Alfred J. Hernandez of LULAC.

When the president joined the group about 8 p.m., he shook everyone's hand, sat down, talked about growing up with Mexican Americans, and said, "Tell me your complaints and problems. I want each of you to talk to me." The participants were not shy. They pressed the president for responses to a litany of problems. They also spoke to the need for more strategic institutional responses to their concerns, suggesting that LBJ create a special federal committee to work on such issues.

According to Bert Corona,

> the president's advisors . . . liked the idea of a federal specific committee . . . but felt . . . that a special White House committee would have only short-range impact. What they wanted—and LBJ concurred—was an interagency, cabinet-level committee that would be more permanent and could play a more effective role with departments such as Health, Education, and Welfare and the Labor Department. They agreed to establish a working committee, including Mexican-American representatives, to formally propose the idea. As a result, the meeting broke up on a positive note. None of us had any illusions about what might come out of the meeting. We knew it would be exploratory, but we were pleased with the concrete results concerning the agency.

For a time a truce was struck between the Mexican-American community and the White House, but developments that followed quickly brought that truce to a halt. After a review of his involvement in the walkout staged at the EEOC's regional meeting in Albuquerque, Forumeer Rodolfo "Corky" Gonzáles was fired from his post as director of War of Poverty youth programs in Denver. Apparently Gonzáles was viewed by White House officials as being too zealous.[21] The firing reactivated fierce criticism of the Johnson administration by community activists. These criticisms were fueled by the president's apparent failure to recollect his commitments to establish an inter-agency committee on Mexican-American affairs and to convene a conference on Hispanic community issues. More than a year passed before any substantive action was taken by Johnson to fulfill these commitments.

During this period, Johnson's presidency lost itself in the marshes of a place called Vietnam. Domestic reaction to building American military involvement in that nation began to reach a pitch surpassing that of the civil rights movement. Johnson's power and personality underwent marked change. In the process, so too did the Mexican-American community undergo marked change. "Corky" Gonzáles began to emerge as one of a handful of new Mexican-American leaders militantly opposed to administration policies pertaining to the Hispanic community. In late 1966, Gonzáles founded the Denver-based Crusade for Justice and began preaching community self-awareness and self-determination. He also began to articulate the growing frustration of *barrio* youths, which liberal American society had largely overlooked in the wake of César Chávez's crusade on behalf of rural *mexicanos*. In this way, Gonzáles began to define the central premises of the Chicano movement, along with emergent community leaders in other regions: José Angel Gutiérrez in Texas, Reies López Tijerina in New Mexico, and Bert Corona in Los Angeles.[22]

The voice and influence of these Chicano leaders resonated with many Forumeers and motivated increasing efforts by Forum leaders to secure administration concessions. In Washington, D. C., Forum activists Rudy Ramos and Raúl Yzaguirre coordinated strong community action against Johnson's delays in responding more systematically to Hispanic needs and to the call for a White House conference. Their efforts to organize Mexican-American community strategy meetings, letter-writing campaigns, and lobbying efforts effectively made clear that *mexicanos* were growing impatient with Johnson.[23]

In Corpus Christi, Hector García himself was growing impatient with administration delays. The blockage of a Forum-sponsored employment and training proposal in LBJ's Labor Department prompted the doctor to meet personally with Johnson in early 1967. García used the occasion not only to unplug the employment program's federal funding, but also to express broader concerns regarding the president's relations with the nation's Hispanics. The meeting had an effect on Johnson. In February 1967 the Forum employment and training program—Operation SER/Jobs for Progress (co-sponsored with LULAC)—was granted $5 million to begin operations.[24] Thereafter, the president took additional steps to bolster his failing relationship with the Chicano community, beginning with the dual appointment of Vicente Ximenes as EEOC commissioner and chairman of the long-awaited inter-agency committee on Mexican-American affairs.

Earlier Johnson promises to organize a White House working committee to plan and formalize the inter-agency group with citizens input never materialized. The press of other commitments probably accounted for this. Consequently, and somewhat surprisingly, Johnson relied almost exclusively on Ximenes to develop the concept. According to Ximenes,

> The president informed me that he wanted to appoint me commissioner to the EEOC. Apparently there had been strong support for me from Dr. García, Louis Téllez (then Forum national chairman), and Zeke Durán (GI Forum state chairman of New Mexico). I really did not want the position, but as usual Johnson was very emphatic about his wishes. He told me he wanted to announce my appointment right away.
>
> Then, he looked me in the eyes and said, "Vicente, I want to do something else, something special, for the Mexican-American people . . . I want to establish a special high-ranking office for Mexican-American affairs. What do you think?"

Ximenes responded that the concept was a good one, but that to be effective, it would have to be given top priority and cabinet-level importance, not just a passing interest. The president concluded,

> Why don't you draw something up for me on it and include (OEO director) Shriver, (labor secretary) Wirtz, (HEW secretary) Gardner, (HUD secretary) Weaver, and . . . include Orville Freeman in there too (Johnson's secretary of agriculture). Get someone over in (presidential aide) Califano's shop to help you draw up a memorandum and get back to me on it as soon as you can, will you?

By the end of the day, Ximenes and the presidential staff had finalized plans for what would later be called the "Inter-Agency Cabinet Committee on Mexican-American Affairs." When Ximenes submitted the finalized memorandum to the president, Johnson commented, "Good, we can make the announcement when we swear you in as

EEOC Commissioner. I'll want you to be my chairman for this committee, Vicente."

With the dual announcement of the appointments on June 9, 1967, Ximenes was charged with the indelicate responsibility of bringing to the Johnson administration a greater priority and cognizance of Hispanic concerns in the midst of building opposition to the president from all directions. Yet the opportunity was formidable and unprecedented. With critical input and assistance of GI Forum members around the nation, Ximenes set out to meet the challenge.

The first order of business was to pursue the yet unanswered call for a presidential conference. Ximenes quickly mobilized support to organize a series of cabinet-level hearings in El Paso, Texas, to coincide with the president's scheduled signing of an international border agreement with Mexican president Díaz Ordaz.[25] Ximenes' Inter-Agency staff was given full responsibility to organize the hearings, and it rapidly mobilized national Hispanic leadership to assist. GI Forum national and state leaders played particularly significant roles in shaping the program's content.

Polly Baca Barragán, Ximenes' chief information officer in the White House (a long-time Forumeer and later a Colorado state senator), also played a major role in putting the hearings together. Baca Barragán was principally responsible for all publicity and public relations attendant to the staging of the hearings. She recalls that the event required a massive logistical effort:

> After the decision was made to hold the hearings we really had only five weeks to put them together, and there was simply an overwhelming number of arrangements that needed to be made. This created some problems. For instance, over 3,000 invitations were extended to prospective participants. Just deciding who to invite created a dilemma for us because we did not want to leave anybody out, yet we could only accommodate so many people. Then there were bureaucratic problems of trying to arrange the various cabinet members' schedules through each of their respective staffs, and then trying to make it all fit in with the president's scheduling. It was not an easy event to organize.[26]

Indeed, there were formidable difficulties encountered in staging the hearings. Besides the logistical problems Ximenes' staff confronted, political problems emerged. State Department officials were outraged by the decision to hold the hearings at the same time as the treaty signing. The State Department worried about the event's potential to insult Mexican officials by distracting from the treaty ceremonies (not to mention overshadowing the department's own efforts and objectives). Several attempts were made by the State Department to convince the president to postpone the cabinet hearings, but Johnson remained content with the planned coordination of events. Finally, though still unsuccessfully, officials at State began opposing the agenda on grounds that the possibility of violent demonstrations at the cabinet meetings created a national security problem.[27]

Opposition within the Mexican-American community mounted as well. Many of the president's increasingly skeptical critics in the Chicano population viewed the hearings in El Paso as proof that Johnson did not feel the problems of Hispanics warranted a White House conference. Moreover, considerable controversy was caused by the conspicuous absence of invitations to more radical and outspoken community leaders such as Reies López Tijerina and César Chávez. According to Polly Baca Barragán, Tijerina was not included because he was then under federal indictment for leading a raid on a courthouse in Tierra Amarilla in protest of the loss of Mexican land grants in New Mexico.[28] The omission of Chávez, clearly the most widely recognized Spanish-speaking leader of the time, was apparently based on a resolve to focus the meetings on *urban* Chicano problems. Louis Téllez, GI Forum national chairman when the hearings were held, later recalled significant concern among the event's planners (himself included) over intense union pressure to use the hearings as a platform to promote the farm-worker agenda. Téllez and others feared that Chávez's involvement would detract from the desired agenda by placing emphasis on union and agricultural concerns.[29]

Whatever the cause, these leaders' absence was taken by many to reflect Johnson's determination not to be embarrassed at the hearings by vocal critics of his policies. This interpretation undermined the legitimacy of the cabinet-level meetings. Numerous of the community's more militant leaders, including Bert Corona, "Corky" Gonzáles, Tijerina, and Ernesto Galarza boycotted the hearings at El Paso and organized a widely publicized protest meeting of their own at the El Paso Hotel del Norte.[30]

The El Paso hearings proceeded nevertheless, with more than one thousand participants including President Johnson, Vice-President Hubert Humphrey, OEO Director Sergeant Shriver, and the secretaries of Agriculture, Labor, Housing and Urban Development, and Health, Education, and Welfare.[31] In fact, this was an unprecedented event in the Mexican-American's long pursuit of justice and equal opportunity. Never before had such a group of high-ranking government officials met outside of Washington with a group of citizens to discuss their problems. Vicente Ximenes, Louis Téllez, Hector García, and others firmly believed that the hearings marked a turning point for the *mexicano* community. According to Ximenes,

> Many of the cabinet members came a little reluctantly perhaps, a little apprehensive about what to anticipate, and a little unsure maybe about why these hearings were necessary. But as witness after witness spoke before the cabinet officials and told their individual stories, you began to see their whole demeanor change. They began to feel a bit more taken by the need for the hearings, perhaps because for the first time, I think, they began to comprehend the level of suffering *mexicano* people were having to endure in this country. I think each of those officials was deeply touched by what they saw and heard at the hearings. Each of them left with a little spark of enthusiasm about new initiatives we might forge on behalf of the people they had come to better understand in El Paso. I think at least they all came away widely in agreement that we in the administration were not doing nearly enough.

Indeed, the El Paso hearings played an important role in convincing policymakers in Washington that more needed to be done. The year that followed the hearings saw important and unprecedented administration initiatives on behalf of Hispanic Americans. The Model Cities program was revamped to include eight predominantly Hispanic cities, and increased administration appointments marked new firsts and broader spheres of influence for Chicanos and other Hispanics. Among the most significant of these was the naming of Dr. Julián Zamora of Notre Dame University to oversee presidential advising on welfare programs, and the selection of Hector García to become the first Hispanic commissioner to the U. S. Commission on Civil Rights.[32] Such gains were complemented by an unprecedented 41 percent increase in Hispanic federal employees over 1965 levels. The number

of these employees earning over the median national income was virtually doubled in 1967. These increases included 9,000 new
Mexican-American employees in the federal labor force throughout the
Southwest; their expanding incomes and benefits extended to an estimated 45,000 family members and their communities.[33] Massive
increases in the federal budget for migrant educational benefits,
employment training and health care for Hispanic Americans, and the
president's signing of the Bilingual Education Act, augmented the
direct benefits received by Hispanics under Johnson. Each of these
gains helped significantly to expand the resources and opportunities
available to U. S. Latino groups.

The years following 1967 saw new outlooks emerge both on and
within the nation's Hispanic population—in government, in private
industry, and in society. These new outlooks translated themselves into
additional gains for Hispanic Americans, many not immediately evident but critical nonetheless. For the first time in history significant
numbers of Chicano and other Latino families began to experience
upward movement into America's middle classes and a closer association with traditional patterns of American mobility. At the same time,
strong attention began being paid to this community's particular bicul-
tural traditions. Special emphasis programs emerged to review testing
biases impeding Hispanic educational progress, to increase the matric-
ulation of Hispanic youth in the nation's colleges and universities, and
to provide public information in Spanish to largely Spanish-speaking
communities. For the first time, really, the nation as a whole finally
began to recognize an important national dimension of race and
inequality extending beyond the relationship between black and white
Americans; now America opened its eyes to the problems of other
identifiable groups of citizens as well.

Clearly, all these changes did not eradicate the many problems and
injustices experienced by Hispanic Americans, but they marked an
important step. The improvements they brought about were real and
significant for millions of people. The GI Forum's contributions to
these changes were considerable and multifaceted. Numerous
Forumeers contributed to the process of change from within the government—Vicente Ximenes, Ed Terrones, Larry Ramírez, Polly Baca
Barragán, and Hector García. Even under the most difficult of circum-

stances, during a uniquely turbulent era in American history, they served their people and their nation admirably. Their efforts helped significantly to secure the many new programs and initiatives that came out of this period.

Other Forumeers contributed as much to the process of change outside of government, through activism and protest. "Corky" Gonzáles, Rudy Ramos, and Raúl Yzaguirre were among those whose activism served both to sensitize mainstream America to the suffering in Hispanic communities, as well as to enhance the consciousness of Hispanics themselves. From such efforts came the popularization of the Chicano's plight, and with it the Chicano movement.

Finally, of course, there were those Forumeers who influenced change during this period through their roles and activities within the GI Forum itself—Anita Campos, Augustine Flores, and Louis Téllez among others. From their contributions came consistency in organizational leadership and continued GI Forum influence, not only at the national level but also in states and localities throughout the nation.

These contributions might have been even greater had it not been for the war in southeast Asia. But Johnson's failure to recognize the imminent dangers of America's role in Vietnam finally prevented him from adequately overseeing his War on Poverty at home. As a result, Chicanos and other minorities in the 1960s were left with the inspiration of a socially ambitious president, but without adequate means to build further towards the Great Society he aspired to create. This was unfortunate, for Lyndon Johnson not only had a greater understanding of *mexicano* problems than any president before him or since, but he also inherited a rare opportunity to forge a path that might have substantially eliminated those problems altogether for many Hispanic groups.[34] Johnson made undeniable strides towards achieving that end, but in the final analysis he fell far short of his own vision.

In the end, the war in Vietnam undid LBJ's own political viability as well as that of the Democratic Party. The result was a Republican presidential victory in 1968 and several uncomfortable years for Chicanos with Richard M. Nixon in the White House. But with many of the most critical political gains secured through groundwork laid in the 1960s, the Forum would turn increasingly in the 1970s with other

Hispanic groups to economic issues, namely, the continuing struggle to ensure freedom of economic and employment opportunity.

Chapter 6

Economic and Employment Struggles

David Vogel's *Lobbying the Corporation* highlights activist America's relative shift in the 1970s from the previous decade's predominantly *political* protests to *economic* demands for business accountability to citizen interests. Writing in 1977, Vogel explained the origins and nature of the corporate accountability movement in this way:

> Traditionally in liberal political thought and practice, only one institution was thought to be responsible for looking after the public welfare—the State. To the extent that the public had common interests and shared common values, it was the responsibility of government officials to articulate and represent them. For in their political roles, as public officials or citizens, individuals were presumed in principle to be motivated by the interests of the commonweal . . . These principles were, of course, routinely breached . . . but they did establish a division of labor that was widely accepted—at least as an ideal. However, during the last fifteen years the corporate accountability movement has challenged them in a number of ways . . . Over the past fifteen years, a new way has been found to influence decisions . . . in the United States. No longer are public demands for change . . . addressed exclusively through government. Instead, a growing number of groups and individuals are taking their criticisms of corporate conduct directly to the firm: they are lobbying the corporation as well as the government.[1]

Many Hispanic groups participated in the generalized current of economic activism during the 1970s, pressuring more vocally than ever before for the enhancement of economic and employment opportunities for Hispanics in the job market and at the workplace. The 1970s, for example, saw Chicano and other Latino groups contribute significantly to the broader minority call for the establishment of far-reaching affirmative action programs in industry as well as in government. Community protest activities aimed at private employers and corporations continuing to discriminate against Hispanics in their business, marketing, and public affairs practices were also growing phenomena during these years. Such activities included not only the wider application of boycott strategies popularized by the farm-worker struggles of the 1960s over wages and working conditions, but also bold new efforts to challenge discriminatory insurance red-lining in places such as East Los Angeles and to open up historically exclusionary private foundations and philanthropic departments of corporations.[2]

Hispanic groups were also increasingly active during this period in opposing insufficient and negative portrayals of Latino people and culture in the mainstream media. According to the National Council of La Raza, studies of Latino media representations during the 1970s underscored the dramatic underrepresentation of Hispanics in American television at that time.[3] Data from the Annenberg School of Communications, for example, shows that between 1969 and 1978 only 2.5 percent of prime-time television characters were identifiably Hispanic, although nearly 7 percent of the U. S. population was Hispanic during those years. Similarly, in a three-season (1975-1978) study of fictional television-series characters, researchers at Michigan State University concluded that "Hispanic Americans are significantly underrepresented in the TV population."[4] Out of a total of more than 3,500 characters, the study found only about fifty Latinos—or 1.5 percent of the total—with speaking roles. Additional inquiries by the Center for Media and Public Affairs reflect that between 1955 and 1986 only 32 percent of the few Latinos who did appear on television were portrayed positively, compared to 40 percent of whites.[5] (By contrast, the Center's data showed that fully 41 percent of Hispanics were portrayed negatively, compared to only 31 percent of whites).

Hispanic community response to the discriminatory practices underscoring these data focused mainly on large corporate advertisers, whose goods and services were relatively more amenable than media networks to minority consumer protests. Thus, Ligget and Meyers, Frito-Lay, Pepsi USA, and the Steck-Vaughn Company were among major corporations whose products, ads, and television commercials were censured by insulted Hispanics during the 1970s. Latino community protests resulted in the demise of such noted media personages as the Frito-Lay Company's "Frito Bandito" and *Papacito and His Family* of Steck-Vaughn publications.

The GI Forum and its individual members were much a part of these emergent endeavors to increase Hispanic opportunities through corporate accountability. Forum chapters in cities and states across the nation both supported the efforts of other groups, as well as initiated their own strategies, to exact private sector responsiveness to Hispanic needs. The Forum's initiatives were necessarily confrontational in most cases. Yet frequently Forum relations with corporate concerns were structured to build new and innovative partnerships between Latino groups and American business and industry. Both of these approaches—the confrontational and the cooperational—had important roles to play in the 1970s, as the Forum sought to promote equality of economic and employment opportunity.

The Forum's greatest contributions to the corporate accountability movement occurred between 1969 and 1979, when it sponsored a nationwide boycott of the Adolph Coors Company of Golden, Colorado, one of the nation's leading beer producers. During this ten-year period, the GI Forum initiated, led, and sustained a powerful challenge to Coors' hiring practices. For urban Chicanos this challenge served the essential consciousness-building function that the farm-worker organizing efforts of the 1960s had served for rural Chicanos. This was particularly the case in the boycott's initial years, when it most mirrored the forces and relationships of the Chicano movement's ideological worldview: a wealthy Anglo employer; systematically disenfranchised and subjugated Chicano workers; growing awareness and resolve to act; perseverance; an increasing sense within the Chicano community of power and, ultimately, of emancipation. Indeed, these were the same forces and relationships the farm worker struggles had made so compelling to the broader community and society. But while urban Chicanos overwhelmingly supported the farm workers and learned much from their experience, the issues that most touched them were different from those of rural Chicanos. Their battles were not in the fields, but in the nation's cities and factories. The Coors boycott constituted a far-reaching initiative, borne out of urban experiences.

The Forum declared the boycott against Coors in early 1969 after nearly three years of Colorado Forum protests over the company's hiring policies were ignored by firm executives. Colorado Forumeers had begun investigating Coors' employment profile and personnel procedures in 1966. At that time, company representatives refused to quote figures on the numbers and positions of minority persons Coors employed. Forum investigators estimated an excessively low total employment of Chicanos at the company and were able to conclude, moreover, that those hired were relegated to the lowest positions.

According to Forum investigations, the primary cause of Chicano underrepresentation was the company's testing requirements of all prospective and hired employees. The tests administered by Coors, called "runner's sheets," were lengthy questionnaires, often requesting highly personal information pertaining to political affiliations and sexual preferences. These tests were followed by a series of interviews measured by polygraph equipment (i. e., lie detectors). Forum leaders contended that the tests were not only excessive and intrusive from a privacy standpoint, but also that their very intent was specifically to discourage the hiring of Chicanos and other minorities.

Chicano opposition to the Coors Company grew during 1968 as GI Forum state chairman Arnold Espinoza's efforts to meet with Coors officials to seek an understanding were denied. When he did finally meet with them, the meetings were unconstructive. In mid-1968, local Forumeers in Colorado began planning the boycott against Coors as a strategy to increase the Forum's bargaining power in negotiating with the company. At the national GI Forum convention at Corpus Christi in August, Espinoza presented a resolution to empower the Colorado state chapter to "use all valid efforts to correct inequitable employment practices . . . by the Adolph Coors Company." In addition, Espinoza asked that the Forum conduct a national campaign to encourage members and supporters to withhold purchases of Coors products if the matter was not resolved by the Forum's next mid-year conference, scheduled for Denver the following February.[6]

Coors officials were apparently unimpressed by the Forum's action. Espinoza's subsequent endeavors to negotiate with Coors officials were met no differently than in the past. Moreover, Coors refused the Colorado Forum's invitation to discuss company hiring issues with Forum national board members at the Forum's February conference in Denver. At that meeting, therefore, the Forum's Colorado delegation reiterated its grievances against the company.

The Forum board established a special task force to negotiate with Coors on a national basis. National Chairman Daniel Campos headed the task force and assigned four others to serve with him: Rudy Ramos, the attorney who represented the Forum in Washington, D. C.; Duven Luján, a personnel relations specialist from New Mexico; Larry Ramírez, past Forum national chairman and equal-employment law specialist from Kansas City; and Colorado State Chairman Espinoza.[7] The task force was charged with demanding prompt and favorable company response to a list of Forum grievances. In the interim, the national Forum body voted to initiate a broad-based, Latino community boycott of Coors products.

Coors officials responded publicly to the boycott by claiming significant increases in the hiring of Hispanic employees in 1967 and 1968. Company announcements in 1969 boasted that 47 of 490 employees hired in 1967 and 59 of 845 employees hired in 1968 were Chicanos (a total of 106 new Chicano employees). But separate official announcements in the same year claimed a total of only 115 Chicano employees out of the total Coors work force of nearly 1,750. Indirectly, then, the company's own accounts reflected that prior to the Forum's complaints beginning in 1967, Coors employed only nine Chicanos in its total labor force of more than a thousand. Moreover, the 1969 company claim of 115 Chicano employees constituted only 6.5 percent of Coors' total labor force, despite a local Chicano population exceeding 10 percent of the total Denver-Golden population. Forum figures reflected that prior to 1967, Chicanos comprised no more than 2 percent of Coors' total labor force. Chicanos were not the only group experiencing discrimination within the Coors Company. African Americans, who made up 7 percent of the total Denver-Golden population, comprised only 1 percent of the total Coors workforce.[8]

With these figures in hand, Forum chairman Dan Campos publicly charged Coors with hiring discrimination and challenged company officials to prove otherwise or dramatically change their policies. Already Campos' special task force had demanded several meetings with Coors executives to resolve the matter. But Coors officials consistently refused to meet with Forum representatives, denying the need for any change. As the boycott gained supporters, Coors' position hardened still further. Company officials became less accessible to Forum and other community representatives, and their demeanor took on an increasingly hostile and defensive character.

In 1970, former GI Forumeer "Corky" Gonzáles, founder of the Denver-based Crusade For Justice, released photographs published by the Crusade's newsletter showing Coors warehouse trucks unloading produce at Denver outlets to assist western growers challenged by striking United Farm Workers union members. The photographs predictably deepened Chicano sentiments against the Coors Company. So did the company's 1969 donation of a surveillance helicopter to the Denver Police Department. Apparently Coors had donated the helicopter to Denver officials out of concern about growing crowds of anti-Coors demonstrators around Coors facilities in Golden and Denver. Indeed the helicopter was subsequently used to tear-gas demonstrating crowds.

Coors' obstinacy mobilized GI Forum chapters and other civil rights groups everywhere. Local and state chapters of the Forum advanced the boycott in their areas by holding press conferences, staging demonstrations, printing public information on Coors' hiring record, and distributing "Boycott Coors" bumper stickers and buttons. The national effort received the support of groups as diverse as LULAC, MAPA, the Crusade For Justice, the NAACP, and the Anti-Defamation League of B'nai B'rith.[9] In Washington, the EEOC filed a federal complaint against Coors' discriminatory hiring policies. The action augmented pending Colorado Civil Rights Commission actions against Coors for the discriminatory dismissal of an employee. In August, 1970, the Colorado Civil Rights Commission officially censured Coors for the employee's firing, which it concluded had been based on racial discrimination.

These actions and the publicity they sparked around the nation lent greater support to the Forum-inspired boycott. Coors beer sales plummeted in each of the boycott's first several years. Nevertheless, company officials did not budge. Following the EEOC complaint against the brewery, Coors officials went to court to block further EEOC access to company records. A lower court initially ruled against the EEOC, but in 1973 the U.S. Supreme Court reversed that ruling. Shortly thereafter, the EEOC commenced a full-scale investigation of Coors' hiring and promotion policies. GI Forum pressure on Coors was intensified under the leadership of four-time National Chairman Antonio Gil Morales.

Subjected by the Supreme Court's decision to official EEOC action—and by the Forum's relentlessness in spreading the bad publicity—the Coors Company began to comply with state and federal equal-employment opportunity laws. By 1975 it appeared that Coors was indeed making good-faith efforts to remedy its longstanding problems. Affirmative action plans began to be mapped out, and an office of liaison to Hispanic groups was developed within the company's community relations department. Furthermore, Coors funding assistance to Latino community organizations (denied altogether during the early years of the boycott) began to increase during the late 1970s, and Chicano (as well as black) faces began to appear in Coors print and television advertising campaigns. By 1977 Coors was among the most visible financial contributors to Latino community causes in the brewing industry's increasingly competitive (and boycott-inspired) outreach efforts to Hispanic consumers.

At the Forum's national convention of 1977 a motion was presented to suspend the Coors boycott, pending the negotiation of a mutually agreeable boycott resolution between Forum national officers and Coors officials. The boycott was not suspended, but an organizational review process was set in motion, under the direction of then California Forum Chairman Jake Alarid, to assess Coors policies and procedures beyond the company's expanding financial expenditures to improve Hispanic community relations. Following extensive reviews, the Coors boycott was officially halted entirely at the Forum's national convention of 1979. The resolution eventually resulted in a landmark $350 million commitment by Coors to support Hispanic community business opporunities and causes under the umbrella of an important new organization called HACR: the Hispanic Association on Corporate Responsibility. HACR members included the American GI Forum, the Cuban American National Council, the National Council of La Raza, the National Puerto Rican Coalition, and the U. S. Hispanic Chamber of Commerce. In subsequent years, HACR has become one of the nation's most influential advocates for corporate responsibility issues affecting U. S. Latino groups.[10]

By any standard, the boycott had been an overwhelming success that had achieved more than its immediate objectives; it had served not only to stem the Coors Company's discrimination in hiring and personnel procedures, but also to broaden corporate recognition of the Forum's potential to successfully challenge industrial giants. In this regard, the Forum-inspired Coors boycott contributed meaningfully to a general increase in business responsiveness to Hispanic groups during the 1970s. Furthermore, the boycott expanded consciousness among disadvantaged Chicanos in cities and towns across the nation that broad-based community action could make a great difference.

While the Coors boycott aptly demonstrates the Forum's ability to exact meaningful economic and employment gains through confrontational community action, confrontation politics were not the only basis of Forum efforts. In fact, the 1970s were years in which the Forum sponsored new community-based programs, which—hand in hand with effective pressure tactics—enhanced Latino economic and employment opportunities by building new partnerships with corporate America. Of these programs, two warrant particular attention: the Forum's role in establishing SER/Jobs For Progress, Inc. as the nation's largest Hispanic employment and training agency, and its subsequent creation of the Veteran's Outreach Program (VOP), to link returning Mexican-American Vietnam veterans to gainful economic and employment opportunities. Both involvements reflect well the GI Forum's continuing contributions to Latino community development and innovation.

In 1964, members of the founding chapters of the GI Forum and LULAC collaborated in the establishment of SER (Service, Employment and Redevelopment) as a voluntary organization providing job training and placement assistance to lower-skilled Chicanos in

Corpus Christi. Two years later the organization received its first federal assistance of $250,000 from the U. S. Department of Labor. This starting grant made it possible for SER to establish an administrative office in Albuquerque, New Mexico. It also supported planning and preparation activities for a regional structure of eleven operating centers to conduct employment training activities targeted to Hispanic communities in five southwestern states.[11] A board of directors was established, composed equally of national GI Forum and LULAC representatives, to direct SER planning and operations.

With its administrative structure and operating plan in place by mid-1966, SER sought program funding for 1967 through U. S. Department of Labor and OEO-administered Manpower Development and Training Act (MDTA) funding. Johnson administrators moved slowly in granting a funding contract, however, largely because Labor secretary Willard Wirtz was not persuaded that SER was necessary. The bottleneck was unplugged in early 1967 when Hector García went to Lyndon Johnson personally to free up sufficient funding for the program. In May 1967, SER received MDTA funding totaling $5 million for the 1967-1968 fiscal year. The regional SER office in Albuquerque quickly unveiled plans to establish training sites in San Antonio, Phoenix, Houston, Denver, and Los Angeles, and to develop a national skills bank designed to assist Hispanic workers in obtaining employment in non-traditional positions.[12] By November of 1968 these goals had been met and new offices were established in El Paso, Texas and San Jose, Santa Clara, Santa Ana, and San Diego, California.

SER's growth and success in ensuing years was phenomenal, due largely to its far-reaching and innovative approaches and outlook. Cognizant that four out of five employment opportunities have traditionally occurred in private industry, for example, SER administrators set out early in the organization's development to establish a corporate advisory body called National Amigos de SER. This advisory council grew to consist of such Fortune 500 representatives as Aetna Life Insurance Company, Ford Motor Company, General Electric, IT&T, Lockheed, Standard Oil, and Union Carbide. Throughout the 1970s the Amigos body served to build new linkages between business and industry and the Hispanic community. For SER, these relationships provided important managerial expertise and funding assistance. Thus the SER network's successful expansion was marked by a healthy mix of public and private sector support. By 1979, SER's 130 programs in 98 cities across the nation were supported by $60 million in contracts provided through expanded government assistance from state and federal agencies, and ever increasing financial agreements with private industry. These contract dollars produced individually structured SER services for Latino men, women, and youth in many areas—on-the-job training, classroom tutoring, career counseling, and business assistance, among others.

SER's marked growth and innovative programs helped to place hundreds of thousands of individuals in meaningful new jobs and careers previously unattainable. As importantly, SER's contributions extended beyond its benefits to SER program trainees and participants, for the organization's expanding network itself provided new opportunities for trustee, managerial, and executive experience never before held on such a wide scale by members of the Hispanic community. In every city and region where SER programs were established, for example, local GI Forum and LULAC members sat on boards of directors to share responsibility for the development of SER policymaking and initiatives. Along with local SER administrators, these individuals wielded direct authority in overseeing the financing, management, and implementation of SER programs within broad organizational parameters. It marked the first time that many of these individuals had ever been afforded the resources and opportunity to influence so directly the developments of their own lives and communities. According to Dr. Clotilde García, a GI Forum representative on SER's first national board of directors,

> SER offered new opportunities for Spanish-speaking Americans, and not only for the men, but also for our women and youths . . . SER opened doors for these people that had never before been opened to them. It was very important especially for helping our poor unskilled workers develop their skills and gain confidence in themselves. SER also gave our people executive positions. We began to see our boys and our young ladies earning middle-income salaries. Our people had never earned those kinds of salaries; they had never been in executive positions as directors or administrators, or chairmen of this or that . . . It was a very special thing for us.[13]

During the 1970s, in the wake of high inflation and unemployment, SER played an especially critical role in ensuring what few gains Latinos were able to make in America's troubled economic and employment arenas. It helped to uplift from the lower end of the nation's economic ladder thousands upon thousands of unskilled Hispanic workers, many of whom were youths, and it defined new horizons for newly skilled Latino managers and administrators, many of whom were women.

Many of SER's strategies and achievements were mirrored a second important GI Forum project in the 1970s—the Veterans Outreach Program (VOP). The VOP was established by the Forum in 1973 to assist Hispanic Vietnam veterans experiencing difficulties re-entering American society and the nation's workforce. The problems confronting these veterans upon their return were great. But many preferred to forget the war, and in doing so they overlooked the trauma of those who had fought for their country. The lack of attention to these veterans' needs was exacerbated by the declining American economy throughout the 1970s, which severely limited the economic and employment options of Vietnam veterans, many of whom had been absent from the labor market for as many as four years.

The VOP proposed to meet the needs of these veterans through an active and innovative outreach program that welcomed the veteran's participation and offered him cost-free, individualized counseling and employment assistance. The U. S. Department of Labor provided initial funding for the Forum to establish eighteen outreach centers throughout Texas and at various locations in the West and Midwest. VOP outreach efforts were vigorous, involving a variety of strategies to identify and assist veterans: street leafleting, door-to-door visits, field counseling, and public service announcements. The VOP developed a wide-ranging list of responsive services for its constituents, including personal counseling, service referral and facilitation, determination of benefits eligibility, job skills analysis, job-search assistance, and employment training and placement.

To improve and expand on these efforts, VOP administrators mobilized strong financial and material support from local Hispanic leaders and civic groups. Beyond this, VOP administrators introduced SER-inspired models of Hispanic community-business partnership to open doors for veterans through the establishment of preferential hiring and training agreements with employers.[14]

The Veterans Outreach Program, and its related support efforts, experienced overwhelming success. During the Program's first fourteen months of operation, for example, its various offices contacted and provided services to more than 30,000 veterans requiring special emphasis assistance.[15] An overwhelming number of these veterans were gainfully employed through their contact with the VOP. Since this bold beginning, thousands of other such veterans have received service and employment assistance through the VOP.

Even more than the Forum's other involvements during the 1970s, the VOP's efforts best reflected the GI Forum's unbending dedication to the very concerns that initially brought about its creation. Only slightly more than twenty-five years preceding the VOP's development, another group of Hispanic veterans had returned from battle to confront similarly formidable circumstances and challenges; even in 1973 those older veterans remembered too well the injustices and contradictions they had faced in their own nation upon returning from duty overseas. In their younger days, they had no recourse to these injustices save the energies of one organization: the American GI Forum. In the end, it was the Forum that had secured their rightful benefits following the war, that brought new hope to secure a better education for their children and greater justice under the law. It was the Forum that secured more representative influence within their nation's political process and that broadened their options within the economy and at the workplace. At the outset of the Forum's journey, its members had committed themselves to uphold and protect their piece of the American dream whenever and wherever it might be challenged by ignorance, hatred, discrimination, or injustice. They had carried this commitment through from leading the Hispanic community during the Felix Longoria affair up to establishing the Veterans Outreach Program.

The creation of the VOP brought the Forum full circle: It reiterated that the organization had grown significantly enough over the years to bring about powerful change; and confirmed that its goals, values, and objectives had remained essentially uncompromised through the process. Indeed, strength and consistency of character were the engines that propelled the GI Forum through its early victories in veterans affairs, education, and civil rights. In the 1970s these qualities inspired new Forum victories on behalf of Hispanic Americans in the economic and employment arenas. In the early 1980s, the same motivating factors would sustain the GI Forum's efforts in an era that experts promised would pose both new challenges and unprecedented opportunities—the "Decade of the Hispanic."

Chapter 7

The "Decade of the Hispanic" and the New Federalism

At the close of the 1970s, *Time* magazine christened the coming decade the "Decade of the Hispanic," a ten-year period that would see Hispanic Americans emerge as the nation's largest minority population and that would expand Latino participation in all aspects of American life.[1] Other publications followed suit in the months thereafter with feature articles and reports on Hispanic groups and issues.[2]

To be sure, the first years of the 1980s witnessed unprecedented coverage of Hispanic names and faces in national events and headlines. Marine sergeants William Gallegos and James López, for example, were among the most canonized of 52 American embassy personnel held hostage and then released by Iranian revolutionaries in Teheran.[3] Entertainers and sports figures, such as singer Gloria Estefan, director and playwright Luis Valdez, actor Edward James Olmos, golfer Nancy López, and World Series-winning pitcher Fernando Valenzuela, gained national recognition and acclaim. And Henry G. Cisneros of San Antonio, Texas, was elected the first Hispanic mayor of one of the nation's ten largest cities.

In Washington, the "Decade of the Hispanic" manifested itself in the form of expanding Latino political presence and influence. A product of the civil rights gains achieved by the GI Forum and other groups in the 1960s, the emergence of Latino policy professionals in Washington during the 1970s—elected and appointed officials, federal employees, lawyers and consultants—facilitated the development of strong new Hispanic lobbying groups. Such groups, which included the Congressional Hispanic Caucus, the National Association of Latino Elected and Appointed Officials (NALEO), the International Mexican American Association of Government Employees (IMAGE), the National Council of La Raza, and the Mexican-American Legal Defense and Educational Fund (MALDEF), provided essential new forums for Hispanic communities to advance their policy interests on such issues as affirmative action, bilingual education, immigration, voting rights, and political representation. Not surprisingly, as America entered the 1980s, the combination of expanding Hispanic political expertise and organizational wherewithal in the nation's capitol helped to establish a stronghold for Latinos in national policy discussions.

At bottom, the Hispanic policy community of the 1970s was essentially independent and nonpartisan. Its principal concern was to promote Latino, rather than partisan, policy gains. On the other hand, under Democratic president Jimmy Carter, Hispanics did relatively well on federal appointments and funding. Access to the White House, to shape important policies affecting Latino communities, was considerably more generous for Hispanic civil rights leaders under Carter than had ever been the case under his predecessors Nixon and Ford, both of whom had strong Latino business backing but lacked community ties. Consequently, throughout the Carter presidency, Latino claims to federal and Democratic party largesse expanded.[4]

As Carter's re-election prospects floundered in the wake of inflation, the Iranian hostage crisis, and Senator Edward M. Kennedy's Democratic primary challenges, Carter sought desperately to consolidate his base wherever and however he could. His appeals to Hispanic voters were especially considerable in the waning days of the 1980 presidential campaigns. In a surprising move, he appointed East Los Angeles labor leader Esteban Torres to head a newly established, cabinet-level office of Hispanic affairs. He also appointed former Los Angeles school board president Julian Nava as America's first Chicano ambassador to Mexico.[5]

These last-minute gestures helped Carter to secure more than 70 percent of the Hispanic vote in the November election. But Carter's presidency was not salvageable. The former Georgia governor was roundly defeated in an historic landslide by the popular conservative California governor Ronald Reagan. Reagan, who took 44 of the 50 states from the incumbent, promised a "New Federalism" that would "return the government to the people." In good measure, Reagan proposed to accomplish this by eliminating large national social programs and entitlements, and by returning fiscal and regulatory control to states and localities. On this platform Reagan carried forward a victory significant enough to give his party not only control of the White House, but also (for the first time in decades) a majority in the U. S. Senate.[6] The combination of Reagan's anti-"big government" philosophy, his overwhelming victory, and Republican control of the Senate would profoundly transform the nation and its policy priorities. The changes this transformation inspired, moreover, would create real and frequent hardships for Hispanic and other minority constituencies during the Reagan presidency.

To conservatives who had elected Reagan, the new president was going to Washington to do their bidding—the launching of a conservative revolution as sweeping and decisive in its way as the liberal New Deal revolution had been a half-century earlier. According to Bob Schieffer and Gary Paul Gates, authors of *The Acting President*,

> The Reagan revolutionaries hit town like a conquering army vowing to repeal the New Deal and to clean out a bureaucracy that they claimed had been peopled for decades with liberal Democrats and moderate Republicans. These firebrands wanted real change and not just at the top. They wanted to reach deep into the government and replace people they saw as faceless, left-leaning Democrats with disciples of the conservative movement, disciples who could survive a Reagan administration as so many New Dealers had survived FDR's.

Most of Reagan's New Federalists, focussing on massive social spending cuts and defense expenditure increases, targeted for elimination civil rights programs that were part of the Great Society. Latino leaders and organizations suddenly found themselves at risk of major setbacks. Few who could speak for these interests, moreover, had access to the new president or important members of his team to advocate for more tempered policy strategies.

However, the GI Forum was able to gain important access to Reagan through key Republicans around him, who were positioned to influence presidential decision-making in critical areas of concern to Hispanic leaders and communities. Ultimately, to the surprise of many, these contacts helped to position the GI Forum as Reagan's most important Latino civil rights adviser during his first term.

The Forum's unique access to Reagan and his New Federalists could not ultimately salvage Latino and other minority constituencies from budget cuts and social policy retrenchments. It did, however, help to modify the nature and extent of administration actions on several important fronts of concern to Hispanic Americans. Much of the credit for this goes to the Forum's newly elected organization leader. In August of 1980 Forum members elected José R. Cano to head the American GI Forum as its national chairman. Cano, who had previously chaired the Forum's Texas chapter, was in some ways an adventurous choice for the organization. He was a moderate Republican who surrounded himself with other moderate Republicans, such as Mario Díaz, then GI Forum Kansas state chairman, and fellow Texan Ed Bernáldez, both of whom would later also become Forum national chairmen. Although the organization was constitutionally committed to nonpartisanship, its members had long been predominantly Democratic as a result of the Forum's close ties to the Kennedy and Johnson administrations. Cano was also disliked by many Forumeers and other leaders for his sometimes single-minded tendency to advance unpopular or otherwise unconventional strategies. Both as Texas GI Forum chairman and as a leading member of the National Hispanic Leadership Conference, Cano had often angered his peers, many of whom considered him brash, unpredictable, impatient, and difficult.[7]

However, the very qualities that made Cano an audacious selection to head the Forum would make him an unusually important and effective national chairman in the early years of the Reagan presidency. His Republican ties would assure him access to key conservative political figures that other Hispanic leaders lacked, precisely when those contacts would prove most essential. In addition, Cano's unusual tenacity would enable him to command the new administration's attention to concerns that might not otherwise have been noticed.

At the end of 1980, Cano began to establish a strong relationship with the new Reagan administration, building on contacts with key

Republican Hispanic staffers on Capitol Hill. These individuals, many of whom had past ties to the Forum, were strategically critical to Cano's agenda, both because of their knowledge of Forum history and because their bosses were senior GOP leaders now slated to head some of Washington's most influential congressional committees. They included Ernie García, a former GI Forum youth member and a leading staff representative of Kansas Senator Robert Dole, who would soon chair the Finance Committee; Bob Estrada, a key staffer for Texas Senator John Tower, who was slated to head the Armed Services Committee; and John Florez, a new staff representative of Utah Senator Orrin Hatch, who would replace Ted Kennedy as chair of the Labor and Human Resources Committee.

Early meetings with these individuals emphasized the Forum's desire to work with the new administration, to ensure that Reagan's New Federalism would realize its many promised economic benefits without undermining policies designed to promote minority rights and opportunities. Built into this position, however, were contradictions which time would make clearer.[8] But the Forum's commitment to engage Reagan's people and policies was real. In a lengthy January 1981 article in the *Forumeer*, José Cano articulated his rationale and program:

> The time has come for Hispanics . . . to take stock that contemporary American . . . priorities have ended for some time the degree of federal responsiveness that for so many years saw Hispanic and other minority communities turn increasingly to the federal government for redress of social, political, and economic disadvantages. Like it or not, the change that is emergent . . . is very real . . .
>
> In the days and months to come, Hispanic America must learn to judge the role and performance of the federal government more astutely. Difficult for many of us to admit—but true—is the fact that numerous of the federally funded programs we have supported in order to improve the living conditions of our people have failed miserably . . .
>
> What our struggle needs now are innovative yet realistic strategies for coping with America's emergent political changes in order to make those changes work on our behalf whenever and wherever possible . . . There is little doubt here that this can be done; but if it is, the accomplishment will necessarily be the result of community-based self-help and development . . . Only in this way will we ever hold federal actors accountable to Hispanic needs in those areas

where we truly require government assistance in order to realize our equal rights and opportunities in American society.[9]

Cano's logic was in fact consistent with established GI Forum traditions. Indeed, in the organization's earliest days, independent self-help initiatives were its hallmark. But the Forum's willingness under Cano to critique federal minority programs and to work with the new national leadership was anathema to many other civil-rights leaders. In large measure, these individuals loathed the massive policy shifts promised by Reagan and were firmly committed to fight them at every turn.

On the other hand, Cano's positions were music to Republican ears. Republican leaders realized that they would need credible Hispanic and other minority partners to see through and sell the sweeping social policy reforms they had in mind. The Forum's predisposition under Cano's leadership to engage and partner with Republicans was a welcome development. Given the inconsistencies of the two sides on sensitive issues such as bilingual education, however, the partnership would not always be easy or mutually gratifying.

As a first move, Cano and other Forum principals met with White House transition-team leaders Alex Armendáriz and Henry Zúñiga. Their primary goal was to ensure that Reagan would meet early in his presidency with a representative group of Hispanic advocates. The effort to meet early with such leaders, Cano argued, would establish a needed forum for dialogue between Reagan and community leaders that would help to mitigate real policy differences. Forum appeals along these lines were reinforced by Republican Hill staffers such as Ernie García and Bob Estrada, with whom Cano enjoyed especially good relations.

Cano also pressed the administration to include, for the first time ever, a Latino in the new presidential cabinet—specifically, an Hispanic education secretary. In correspondence to Edwin Meese, director of Reagan's transition team, Cano made this appeal:

> Given that Hispanic American youth will soon comprise the highest percentage of minority school-age children, it would be most advantageous for our community to have . . . the first . . . Hispanic cabinet member in the Department of Education.[10]

To facilitate Hispanic community dialogue with Reagan, the Forum also developed in the winter of 1980 a comprehensive set of recommendations for the new president. Formulated with the assistance of leading Latino experts (including Francisco Garza of the National Council of La Raza, Dr. Richard Santillán of the Rose Institute for State and Local Affairs, SER National Deputy Director Anthony Gomes, and Veteran's Outreach Program [VOP] director Carlos Martínez), the Forum agenda covered several key topics. These included veteran's affairs and national defense, employment and labor, business and economic development, education, and voting rights and reapportionment.[11]

Forum efforts to push for a Latino education secretary did not bear fruit until Reagan's second term. Instead, Utah Educator Terrel H. Bell was appointed to the post. In fact, although Reagan seriously considered at least two Latinos for his cabinet, the new president's initial selections included no Hispanics. A stern letter to the president from more than twenty Hispanic leaders (including José Cano) on January 7, 1981, lamented:

> This omission represents a severe setback for the aspirations of the Hispanic community. It had been our hope, and indeed our expectation, that at least one Hispanic would serve on your cabinet. This expectation was based in part on statements made during the campaign and on the fact that you come from the state (California) with the highest number of Hispanics in the nation and, therefore, presumably would be more sensitive to the need to make your Cabinet broadly representative . . . [12]

Cano pushed hard for the administration to pay greater attention to Latino groups and issues, reminding key Republicans in private discussions that Hispanic strongholds such as California, Texas, Illinois, New York, and Florida, would be essential to conservative candidates in future elections. Cano also began to make increasingly aggressive jabs at the new administration. In doing so, he hoped to inspire Republican concern about losing Forum and other important Hispanic support early in Reagan's tenure because of premature and unnecessarily radical conservative policy moves. Speaking before a GI Forum women's group in Saginaw, Michigan, for example, Cano contemplated the creation of a national alliance of Latino and black voters to unseat unresponsive candidates in the forthcoming 1982 elections. He also sounded an ominous warning of possible civil unrest in reaction to Reagan's economic proposals.[13]

Forum efforts for an early meeting of Hispanic leaders with the new president paid off. In February of 1981, Cano and a small group of other national Hispanic leaders met with Reagan at a White House luncheon.[14] Also attending the meeting were Vice President George Bush, top officials Edwin Meese and James A. Baker III, special assistant for public liaison Elizabeth Dole, and Education Secretary Terrel Bell.[15]

Over lunch, Cano spoke directly with Reagan on numerous topics and he briefly reviewed the Forum's comprehensive recommendations for administration policy. Recognizing Bell's presence, Cano expressed particular concern about the administration's initial directions in education policy. Invoking the Forum's official motto, "Education Is Our Freedom and Freedom Should Be Everybody's Business," Cano specifically lamented Reagan's predisposition to undo national bilingual education programs. Already, Reagan staff had indicated the president's intention to consolidate national bilingual education support into unrestricted block grants to states and localities.

Only days before, Cano had held a press conference in Dallas to criticize Bell's early decision to rescind standing federal requirements designed to facilitate the provision of bilingual education programs.[16] At the press conference, and in discussion with Reagan, Cano highlighted the opportunities that block grants and national regulatory withdrawal would create for states and localities to diminish or end their bilingual services to minority language students (Olivera 1981).

Reagan and Bell reassured Cano and other attending Hispanic leaders that the new administration would uphold existing laws and regulations. Cano and the others knew, however, that early official pronouncements on the subject did not bode well. In effect, these pronouncements had reinforced longstanding Latino suspicions that Reagan was essentially unsupportive, if not hostile, where bilingual education was concerned.

During the balance of the meeting, Reagan assured Latino leaders that his administration would incorporate Hispanics in key jobs and policy considerations. He also requested their support of the Reagan economic reform agenda. Reagan admitted that his plans would require short-term sacrifices by all Americans, but he argued that the required sacrifices would be in the entire nation's longer-term best interests.

Following the meeting, José Cano emphasized his optimism about the long-term prospects for Hispanic leaders to develop constructive relations with the administration. For the time being, however, he neither endorsed nor opposed Reagan's economic reform plan. Instead, he took a wait-and-see approach:

> I think our community will and should continue to closely monitor the administration's decisions and proposals in order to ensure that Hispanics are dealt a fair shake in the wake of the dramatic changes we see forthcoming. Until we see more solid guarantees . . . that our people will benefit, it will be difficult to extend our full-fledged support for the president's economic proposals . . . On the other hand, this doesn't mean that our support for the plan is not at some point possible . . . Of course, we want what is best for the country.

Cano's preparedness to leave the door open for possible future support of the president's program increased his appeal to administration insiders. Such individuals, including White House Chief of Staff Jim Baker, were persuaded that the Forum would at least give the president's program the benefit of the doubt, which few other civil-rights groups were prepared to do.

During the remainder of 1981, Forum dialogue and relations with the nation's new leadership deepened. Organizational interaction with Dole and Tower advanced the Forum's strong interest in securing Reagan's serious consideration of qualified Latinos for key administration posts. In fact, several important Hispanic appointments were secured with greater or lesser degrees of Forum support, including those of Michael Cárdenas (Director, Small Business Administration), Katherine Ortega (United States Treasurer), Ernie García (Deputy Assistant Secretary of Defense), Dr. Cecilia Aranda Franz (Deputy Assistant Secretary of Education), and former National Forum Chairman Tony Gallegos (Commissioner, Equal Employment Opportunity Commission).

In June, Reagan invited Cano to attend a state luncheon at the White House in honor of Mexican President José López Portillo. En route by plane from his home in Dallas, Cano chatted with Texas

Republican Governor William P. Clements, Jr. Cano expressed his fear that Hispanic and black groups would be hurt by the block-grant strategy, and he appealed to Clements to encourage the administration to rethink its plans.[17]

At Orrin Hatch's invitation, Cano testified in July before the Senate Labor and Human Resources Committee in support of relaxing the affirmative action requirements of federal contractors under the U. S. Department of Labor-administered executive order 11246.[18] Arguing that the substantial planning and reporting requirements of the order were unwittingly reducing employer incentives and goodwill to hire minorities and women for federal contracting projects, Cano urged the committee to reform the order's implementation. First, he argued that more emphasis needed to be placed on the "bottom line": the hiring of qualified minority and female employees. Specifically, Cano called for the development of technical assistance capacity at the Office of Federal Contract Compliance Programs (OFCCP), which would help employers to identify effective strategies to expand the diversity of their work forces. According to Cano,

> Technical assistance programs . . . have been directed to showing employers how to compute mathematical gyrations and have served only to fill the pockets of consulting firms and attorneys . . . [T]he technical assistance programs we have in mind would be directed to showing employers ways to meet the "bottom line" . . . Voluntary, industry-wide approaches, including recruiting techniques, scholarships, upward mobility and other programs, would be researched and promoted by OFCCP . . . Industry would be guided towards compliance in a voluntary and creative manner.

Cano also encouraged the committee to eliminate the most burdensome and unproductive reporting requirements of executive order 11246, except as a punitive and remedial measure for employers in gross non-compliance with federal requirements. Finally, he urged the committee to cut back OFCCP's sanctioning authority, which Cano argued fell more logically in the Equal Employment Opportunity Commission's domain.[19]

This testimony substantially informed affirmative-action policy through OFCCP during the Reagan years. It did not sit well, however, with other civil-rights organization leaders, who saw it as an affront to regulatory machinery they had long toiled to create. One especially vocal detractor was LULAC Executive Director Arnoldo S. Torres. In a private discussion with Forum staff following Cano's appearance before the Senate committee, Torres characterized Cano as a "traitor" and a "sellout"[20] for having taken the positions he did.

The 1981 GI Forum national convention in Dallas confirmed the Forum's standing in GOP power circles. Republican speakers and dignitaries in attendance included Jim Baker, Clements, Tower, presidential special assistant Diana Lozano, Ernie García, and Reagan's newly designated Latino ambassador to Uruguay, Tomás Aranda. Speeches by, and private meetings with, these individuals at the convention conveyed the sense of an evolving partnership.

In response, Texas Democrats such as Senator Lloyd M. Bentsen and House Majority Leader Jim Wright, in their own addresses to convention-goers, warned of Republican "smoke and mirrors." Hector García, unable to attend the proceedings due to a longstanding illness, wrote a passionate address to Forumeers, which was featured prominently in the Forum's 1981 convention brochure; it quietly underscored inconsistencies between Reagan's agenda and traditional Forum commitments.

> I hope the organization continues to work for the poor, the uneducated, the elderly, and the suffering. During this year and other years to come, [government] programs for the poor will be cut. I foresee more suffering, more hunger, and less education for our people. I foresee efforts to completely eliminate bilingual education. We must not permit this to happen.[21]

To clarify the organization's moderate position, Cano, in a strong public performance midway through the convention, spoke to growing Latino community ambivalence over Reagan policy at a well-attended press conference.[22] Citing Hispanic community feelings that the president's proposals would disproportionately subject minorities to hardship, Cano qualified the Forum's willingness to support the Reagan economic plan:

> We make it clear now, as we have throughout Mr. Reagan's tenure in office, that we will hold his administration accountable to ensuring equal opportunity for Hispanics to the benefits his program aims at . . . We will do our part as all other proud members of

American society to give the program fair consideration and support wherever possible. But, to the extent that our people are served disparately and unequally to our detriment, we will make our opposition plain and clear. And this will remain our position.

During the next two years, Latino leaders were given cause to question the wisdom of Reaganomics. The American economy tumbled for a time into its worst recession since the Great Depression. Unemployment rates, business failures, and the federal deficit spiraled. In 1982, the percentage of U.S. Latinos in poverty was higher than it had been in 1972.[23]

The effects of government social spending cuts were also made clear. Hispanic national organizations, which had historically provided needed support and assistance to Hispanic communities with federal financing, were suddenly themselves thrown into a fiscal tailspin. The National Council of La Raza (NCLR), for example, experienced a 70 percent budget reduction owing to government cuts in community economic development training and technical assistance, as well as education, health, and other programs key to the Council's service portfolio. SER experienced a 60 percent budget hit, owing to the elimination of CETA (The Comprehensive Employment and Training Act) and cuts of other job training and employment development programs.[24]

Some small gains were achieved. Facing strong pressure from the Forum and other Latino groups, for example, the administration refrained from including bilingual education programs in its federal block-grants plans.[25] In addition, the VOP budget was spared from significant cuts by Department of Labor and Veterans Administration policymakers.[26] On balance, however, few tangible accomplishments were seen, as Reagan turned his attention increasingly from domestic affairs to foreign policy concerns, particularly in Central America.

Redirecting Forum support efforts from the government to the private sector, Cano and other Forum leaders initiated a business and industry advisory council, to generate new contacts with and raise funds from corporate America. Members of the council included executives of Sears, Roebuck & Company, the Gulf Oil Corporation, the American Gas Association, Hewlett-Packard, Montgomery Ward, and the Adolph Coors Company. During the group's first year of activity,

1981-1982, it generated $125,000 in support for Forum national program activities.[27]

Behind the scenes, Cano encouraged the president to give national Hispanic leaders another opportunity to meet with him face to face, to discuss issues of mutual concern. Working especially through Tower, Dole, and Hatch, Cano's appeals to Reagan were forceful and persistent. In early 1983, administration officials informed Cano that Reagan would attend the Forum's 35th annual national convention, scheduled for August, in El Paso. The president's participation at the convention would set the stage for a critical exchange between Reagan and key Hispanic power brokers. It would also constitute another historic landmark in the GI Forum's rich experience; never before had an American president publicly addressed a Mexican-American community organization. Reagan's agreement to speak at the El Paso convention would make the Forum the first such group to hold the distinction of hosting a chief executive.

The 1983 GI Forum convention in El Paso inspired nearly as much internal community debate as had Lyndon Johnson's 1968 hearings on the same topics in the same city fifteen years earlier. Even before Reagan's arrival in El Paso, several acrimonious exchanges were registered in the media between Democratic party principals and Forum officials over Reagan's participation at the convention. One of the major critics of Reagan's visit was Polly Baca Barragán, the longtime Forumeer who had helped to organize President Johnson's 1968 El Paso hearings. As vice-chairwoman of the Democratic party's national executive committee, Baca Barragán suggested that José Cano was not setting "the proper tone" for the Forum by inviting Reagan. "The rank and file membership will vote for the people who have traditionally supported Hispanics [i.e., Democrats]," said Baca Barragán. "They are not going to be fooled by a last minute pitch from a Republican."[28]

Similar criticism was publicly expressed by Patricia Roybal-Sutton of the Texas Democratic executive committee. Roybal-Sutton said that Reagan's "policies are clearly unacceptable to Hispanics, especially because he has cut back protections for minorities and stepped up U. S. involvement in Central America."[29] The state's Democratic leader charged that some GI Forum leaders were simply seeking self-promotion and favor among Republicans at the Latino community's expense.

Speaking to Forumeers on the eve of Reagan's arrival in El Paso, newly elected Texas Democratic Governor Mark White called the president's policies "anti-Hispanic." White went on to characterize Reagan as being:

> out of touch with reality, even though he is trying desperately to show he has some feeling . . . no amount of last-minute rhetoric and eleventh-hour grandstanding can hide the facts . . . [S]ince the Reagan administration took office in 1981, Mexican-Americans have gone on picking lettuce and all the Republicans have done is pick your pockets.[30]

Forum leaders responded forcefully, characterizing such criticisms as partisan bickering that did nothing to further the Hispanic cause. EEOC Commissioner Tony Gallegos, a former GI Forum California state chairman and later national Forum chairman, called Democratic criticisms of the Forum "slander."[31] José Cano reponded that Democratic detractors were "putting up a smoke screen to cover the fact that not one of the [1984] Democratic presidential candidates came to [the Forum] Convention." Cano went on to observe:

> I sense a fear in some of the Democratic leaders that there might be an erosion of their influence in the Hispanic community . . . It's like buying a car—we are going to shop around . . . [We] want answers; and if we don't get them we are going to write some people off . . . It is a waste of time for the governor to tell me what Republicans haven't done for us instead of what he is doing for us.

Against this tumultuous backdrop, Air Force One landed at Biggs Army Airfield at 5:15 p.m. on August 12, for a scheduled private meeting with Forum and other national Hispanic community leaders. The meeting, organized by Cano, included Raúl Yzaguirre of NCLR, William Velásquez of the Southwest Voter Registration Education Project (SVREP), and Joaquín Ávila of MALDEF. Hector García and the Forum's officers also participated, as did White House Chief of Staff Jim Baker and presidential aides Michael Deaver, Craig Fuller, and Cathi Villalpando (who would later serve as U. S. Treasurer).

During the meeting Cano and others expressed the community's sense of need for the president to do more for Hispanic interests. Cano specifically pressed Reagan to afford Latinos greater access at the White House. Cano also challenged the president to make his next cabinet appointment an Hispanic. GI Forum women's leader Maxine Rodríguez expressed concern to Reagan about community perception that his policies were insensitive to the needs of minority women. Raúl Yzaguirre lamented the administration's absence of analysis in weighing budget-cutting options directed to "dependency-creating" versus "opportunity-focused" programs for Hispanic and other groups. Joaquín Ávila implored Reagan to oppose employer sanctions provisions of the controversial Simpson-Mazzoli immigration reform bill, then pending consideration in Congress.[32]

Reagan's responses to the various issues raised were friendly, but oftentimes incongruous to Latino community sentiments and frequently informed (or misinformed, as some saw it) by anecdotal reflections on his experience with Hispanic groups and issues as California governor. "He seemed to fumble and ramble," NCLR's Yzaguirre later told the *Los Angeles Times*, for example. "He told a great many stories and told them well," Yzaguirre added, "but we are very disappointed at his policy by anecdote."[33] In a private discussion following the meeting, SVREP's Velásquez told GI Forum founder Hector García and others that he was not surprised by Reagan's miscalculation of Latino needs, but was seriously taken aback by Reagan's "ignorance." García responded to Velásquez's remarks with a frown.[34]

Reagan's remarks the next day to a polite crowd of over two thousand Forumeers enabled the convention to close on a more positive note. Referring repeatedly to the patriotic military service and accomplishments of Hispanic Americans, Reagan's speech paid special tribute to Hector García[35] and reassured Forumeers that they had a friend in the White House. "I don't have to tell you, the struggle against discrimination is never over," the president acknowledged, adding "this administration will stand by you as you continue your struggle."[36]

To underscore his comments, Reagan announced that a significant new permanent exhibit would be established at the Pentagon, at his request, to honor the contributions of Hispanic veterans to U. S. history and progress. Then, in a momentous and unexpected policy shift, Reagan for the first time ever publicly stated his commitment to support effective bilingual education programs for Hispanic and other language-minority children.

"If there is anything the GI Forum has contributed to in the past several years that will leave a lasting imprint," José Cano would later remark, "it is our contributions to Reagan's public repositioning on bilingual education."[37] In Cano's estimation, President Reagan's statement ensured that, to be viable, American political leaders of all stripes would now be compelled to acknowledge and appeal to language-minority voters and interests in national policy discourse. Time would show these to be the overarching impacts of the American GI Forum's engagement with Ronald Reagan during his first term in the White House.

Summing up at the close of the 1980s, Chicano historian Juan Gómez-Quiñones expressed this dismal perspective:

> The Reagan era was a period of selfish emphasis, jingoism and chauvinism, and a lack of access. The number of persons in a poverty status increased. The Reagan administration was not only inaccessible; it was generally negative toward the basic social and economic needs of the community . . . Both antiworker and antiunion policies impacted on the Chicano community. But also affected were middle class organizations; their funding suffered and their activities were adjusted accordingly.

In fact, however, the Reagan years were not without significant victories where the Forum and Latino community interests were concerned. GI Forum efforts to influence presidential appointments of Hispanics to important federal posts, for example, were not inconsequential. Nor were Forum efforts to inform and moderate the impact on Latinos of Reagan's first term policies.

It is arguable that absent the GI Forum's efforts, Reagan's second term would never have seen the appointment of Lauro Cavazos, an Hispanic, to serve as the U. S. Secretary of Education. It is also probable that without GI Forum pressure Reagan never would have publicly revised his longstanding opposition to federally supported bilingual education.[38] These developments warrant a degree of appreciation. In effect, they changed the terms of political discourse in America by tying the conservative Reagan agenda with certain baseline Latino interests—a place at the presidential policy-making table and in the

American classroom, thereby establishing a new threshold for U.S. Latino civic participation.

Less visible Forum activities undertaken during 1980-1983 warrant appreciation as well. Organizational efforts to protect Latino veterans' programs, to influence responsible redirection in federal affirmative action contracting policy, to expand corporate social-responsibility initiatives, and to ensure continuing dialogue between the Reagan administration and Latino community leaders were important and distinctive in their own right.

The years 1980 to 1983 were difficult for U. S. Latino groups and issues, to be sure. Nevertheless, these were important and productive years for the Forum, years in which its contributions to Latino advancement were real and meaningful. In the end, these contributions helped Forumeers and other Hispanic Americans to promote and advance, even against a prevailing backdrop of federal government retrenchment, the so-called "Decade of the Hispanic."

Chapter 8

Summing Up

In many respects the American GI Forum's hard-fought efforts during 1980-1983 to secure whatever could be attained for Hispanic community groups under Ronald Reagan's New Federalism constituted a last hurrah for the organization. In the years since then, unfortunately, a variety of factors have substantially reduced the Forum's impact in U. S. national policy making. First, its leadership capacities have diminished dramatically as aging leaders of the 1950s, 1960s, and 1970s have failed to attract and retain new talent and younger membership. This has undercut the Forum's relevance to emergent Latino professionals and the broader Latino community's burgeoning youth population. Second, the Forum has failed to initiate needed internal improvements to bolster its management and development capacities; consequently, it has failed to stay ahead of standard developments in modern organizational administration, required to conduct meaningful business with big government, the mass media, and significant corporate and foundation funders.

This combination of leadership and institutional stagnation has arguably dimished the Forum's sense of institutional direction and purpose. Since the early 1980s, the Forum increasingly has been criticized by community observers for its allegedly diminishing community relevance and impact.[1] At the 1985 national convention in San Antonio, the city's charismatic mayor, Henry Cisneros, reminded his audience of the GI Forum's rich history and accomplishments, but he also constructively challenged Forum leaders to refocus their efforts on addressing community problems and needs. The Forum's leadership has focused increasingly on conventions and social events rather than community activism.

For such reasons, the Forum has come to be substantially over-shadowed by national Latino professional organizations such as the National Council of La Raza (NCLR), Mexican-American Legal Defense and Education Fund (MALDEF), and the National Association of Latino Elected and Appointed Officials (NALEO), which have effectively concentrated their activities in selected areas of expertise and specialization. Forum leaders of recent years, have remained essentially grassroots civil-rights generalists.

Gratefully, however, the past years have not detracted from the GI Forum's continuing value on several important fronts. Forum advocacy efforts on behalf of Latino veterans of the U. S. armed forces remain today as timely and essential as they ever have been. Veterans programs administered by the Forum's VOP, for example, continue to provide solid and needed services to Latino ex-servicemen; and recent VOP initiatives to expand into new areas such as affordable housing, business development, and other income- and job-generating activities appear to be promising.[2] Furthermore, Forum public information and education efforts before Congress and other important decision-making bodies continue to elevate official recognition of Latino veterans' special needs in areas ranging from treatment for combat-related post-traumatic stress disorder to inclusion in federal statistical surveys.[3]

In addition, the Forum's involvement in leading national and regional consumer rights coalitions, such as HACR and the Greenlining Institute (which negotiate mutually beneficial contracting and community investment pacts with large U. S. companies and financial institutions), builds logically and effectively on its significant earlier involvements in the corporate social responsibility movement.[4] In 1984 HACR negotiated a five-year agreement involving the Coors Company that committed Coors to up to $350 million in Latino advertising contracts, distributorship agreements, nonprofit organizational contributions, and youth education scholarships.[5] Subsequent agreements with other large U. S. firms, including the Chrysler Corporation, have been even more beneficial to Latinos.

Many state and local GI Forum chapters continue to play important civic leadership roles and to promote needed dialogue between local elected officials, business leaders, and grassroots Hispanic constituencies. Even today, opportunities to participate in local civic affairs are meaningful and important to Latino communities in which the GI Forum remains relevant and active.

Much more significant than all of this, however, is the continuing importance and community educational value of the GI Forum's impressive civil rights history. From this history older and younger Latinos alike—as well as other Americans—can learn from and take pride in the many contributions that postwar Hispanic Americans have made to the nation's political integrity and social progress.

Leading historians agree that the work and leadership of Mexican-American World War II veterans was pivotal to Latino civic and political advancement in the postwar era. These veterans organized one of the most important Hispanic movements for civil rights, gaining unprecedented national recognition and institutional accommodation. Their efforts were informed by a painful history of discrimination and subjugation, which could be effectively challenged only through community advocacy and organization. According to historians Matt S. Meier and Feliciano Ribera:

> The organizing vitality among Chicanos in the Southwest after World War II was supplied by veterans. These second generation Americans, children of migrants who had come to the United States in the 1920s, had learned how the American system functioned[,] how society could be influenced for change . . . Mexican-American veterans of World War II, having had their hopes raised, refused to submit to the discrimination of the prewar era. Often denied their civil liberties and excluded from full participation in American life, they were determined to address issues of cultural, racial, and economic prejudice that had held them in subjugation . . . They struggled for meaningful political representation, ethnic tolerance, and cultural pluralism, and rallied fellow Mexican-Americans to their cause.[6]

The American GI Forum was at the forefront of this work, providing (as Estrada, *et al.*, have observed), "the foundation for attempts to improve the condition of the Mexican people [in the United States]."[7]

It is important for future generations to know that the GI Forum substantially informed twentieth-century changes in Latino political outlook and community activism. In its golden years, the Forum helped to make the American dream a reality for significant and unprecedented numbers of Hispanic people. It developed a new order of Latino community leadership and strategy. It helped to expand Hispanic community access to public services, social opportunities, and political rights by dramatically increasing community participation in public and civic affairs. It introduced massive voter-registration campaigns. It filed and won landmark lawsuits to remedy systemic violations of civil rights. It fought to desegregate public schools and facilities. It helped to position Latinos as meaningful participants in national policy formation and debate. Employing patriotic rhetoric and symbols, the Forum created a secure position from which to defend Latino rights and to demand reforms during times when anything considered foreign was suspect.

Today these efforts and contributions are easy to underestimate. Some, unfortunately, may even take them for granted or see them as irrelevant to present-day concerns. It is especially difficult for younger observers to comprehend fully how much the Forum was once called upon to change the face of American society for the better—to shift the paradigm of Latino possibilities, for the balance of the twentieth century and beyond.

We know from history, however, that paradigm shifts do not occur in a vacuum; they require contextual origins, hard-working agents of change, and a visionary sense of some different and fundamentally better future. In this sense, paradigm shifts governing social progress are best seen as steps on a long and arduous path. Each step in the process leads to something better. To understand ourselves and our possibilities in this context, it is necessary to understand our antecedents, their lessons, and the implications of those lessons for the future. This is the challenge and responsibility of every generation.

Among the most significant antecedents of contemporary Latino community organizations is the American GI Forum. Through the continuation and deepening of the Forum's work, the concept and the reality of the American dream are made more concrete and accessible to countless millions of Latino people in the United States. In the process, our nation's democracy and its prospects for long-term survival and prosperity are substantially enhanced; so too is our sense of ourselves as Americans.

Epilogue

On July 26, 1996, Hector P. García, the American GI Forum's founder and guiding spirit, died of pneumonia and congestive heart failure. He was 84. His death in Corpus Christi followed years of debilitating illness and a long stay at Memorial Medical Center.[1]

Commentary and reflection on the doctor's legacy abounded in the months leading up to and following his death. On June 21, President Bill Clinton phoned García to wish him well after learning of his failing condition at a meeting with GI Forum National Chairwoman Alma Riojas Esparza.[2] Clinton had known García for years, dating back to Clinton's work on George McGovern's presidential campaign in 1972, at which time he visited with the doctor and members of the American GI Forum at García's home. Upon news of García's death, Clinton recognized the doctor as a national hero in a statement that read in part: "Dr. García fought for half a century for the civil and educational rights of Mexican-Americans . . . Hillary and I extend our deepest condolences to his family . . ."[3]

In a special *Hispanic* magazine article published earlier in the year, GI Forum national executive director Tony Morales had aptly commented:

> Dr. Hector P. García raised the consciousness of our community like no one else has. It was his motivation, his inspiration, that caused the community to start being more [aware of things] happening . . . We can attribute to him the work that many individuals did in later years because when he was organizing the American GI Forum there was a complete vacuum in organizational leadership in our commu-

nity . . . no other group . . . was even talking about the issues García undertook.[4]

A July 29 rosary vigil and formal burial services on July 30 drew an estimated 2,000 mourners. According to the *Corpus Christi Caller-Times*, many of them wore blue and red GI Forum military-style caps trimmed with gold. Many spent long moments in front of García's casket, which was draped with an American flag. Some could not walk unattended. The audience included the well-known and the obscure, powerful politicians and Hispanic leaders a generation removed from the struggles that propelled García into national prominence.[5]

Dignitaries attending García's services included Texas Attorney General Dan Morales, U. S. Representative Solomon Ortiz, Texas State Senator Carlos Truan, Texas State Representative Hugo Berlanga, Texas A&M University-Kingsville President Manuel Ibáñez, and National Council of La Raza president Raúl Yzaguirre—all individuals whose accomplishments and positions Hector García's life and work had helped to make possible.

Yzaguirre interrupted attendance at the Olympic Games in Atlanta to attend the funeral. "It was impossible for me to stay away," said Yzaguirre in a local press interview. "Dr. Hector is most responsible for me being part of the movement. He inspired me . . . to a cause, to meaning in my life." Yzaguirre had organized GI Forum youth groups throughout Texas in the late 1950s.[6]

Texas Attorney General Dan Morales also recalled his experiences with García. "Dr. García was one of the first people I visited with about my . . . aspirations," Morales told reporters. "The best advice he ever gave me was: 'Make sure you never forget where you came from.'" According to Morales, "Dr. García lived his life according to that philosophy."

Former Corpus Christi mayor Luther Jones, donning the distinctive red and blue GI Forum cap, told reporters that García's passing, though somber, afforded an important opportunity for all to reflect positively upon "the changes he helped make in Corpus Christi, Texas and in the entire nation." Summing up the doctor's legacy, Jones observed further that the Forum's deceased founder was "an example of what an individual can do to make a difference."

García's nephew, J. A. "Tony" Canales, a former U. S. attorney, commented to the press that Hector García "represented the pure concept of volunteerism. He had no ulterior motives. He never ran for office and he never made any money off of what he did." According to Canales, "Dr. Hector died poor in financial resources, but rich with friends."

Lena Coleman, president of the local NAACP chapter in Corpus Christi, commented to local reporters that García "did good things for people, not only in south Texas but all over. He was a civil rights leader for all of the people. We lost a great person."[7]

On Monday evening, July 29, García's body was placed in state on the stage of Selena Auditorium at Corpus Christi's Bayfront Plaza Convention Center. A series of large American flags adorned the stage. An honor guard of GI Forum members flanked the doctor's casket. A steady stream of mourners walked past García's body from 10 a.m. until 6:15 p.m., when the Corpus Christi Veterans Band began a musical tribute. The tribute included a stirring rendition of "The Battle Hymn of the Republic," one of García's favorite pieces. Vietnam veteran Greg Mendoza concluded the tribute by singing "The Star-Spangled Banner." Mendoza's rendition of the national anthem brought participants to their feet. Hats were removed. Hands were placed over hearts or raised in salute. As Mendoza's voice filled the hushed facility, a giant flag that had flown over the battle carrier *USS Lexington* slowly unfurled behind García's casket. Following the formal program, the procession of mourners past the casket continued through the night.[8]

The following day more than twenty local police officers and sheriffs filled the motorcade route to escort Hector García's remains to burial.[9] Those who attended García's funeral were of all races, religions, and ages. Some dressed in expensive suits, others in guayaberas; some wore sandals, others cowboy boots.

Robert Parks, a local high-school history and government teacher, brought his camera to García's burial mass. He wanted pictures to use in a portfolio to teach his students about the doctor's legacy. "He was a national figure," Parks told reporters. "He fought for the rights of everybody, and that's why I admired him . . . He was a good man with a good heart."[10]

Two hours before the funeral service's commencement, people filed into Corpus Christi's Catholic cathedral. Pews filled quickly. Some people stood at the rear of the cathedral. The streets surrounding the cathedral were jammed with parked cars that would follow the funeral procession to Seaside Memorial Cemetery.

Religion and patriotism blended seamlessly throughout the funeral mass. American flags fluttered outside the church. A GI Forum banner hung just to the left of the cathedral altar. Eighty singers from the cathedral's pontifical choir, accompanied by youth chorale singers and members of the Corpus Christi symphony, performed musical selections ranging from "Amazing Grace" to "America the Beautiful."

As the service concluded, GI Forum members filed out of the church, followed by García's coffin and his family. A drummer with the Corpus Christi Veterans Band played a stoic military funeral cadence as pallbearers brought the flag-covered casket down the cathedral steps.

Several hundred cars made up the funeral procession from Corpus Christi cathedral to Seaside Memorial Cemetery. The six-mile route took about twenty minutes to travel. Thirty-two American flags lined the cemetery's main entrance. For more than an hour before the procession's arrival, people had been gathering by the hundreds at the burial site. As the motorcade entered the cemetery, GI Forum members stood at attention between each fluttering U. S. flag.

At the gravesite, family members and special guests were escorted from their cars to a shaded graveside pavilion. Hector García's widow, Wanda, sat between her two daughters, holding a crucifix and a white rose on her lap. Various family members, including the doctor's brother Xico and his daughter Cecilia, spoke briefly and simply about García's extraordinary life and work. Then, at the funeral's conclusion, Gilbert Cásares, commander of the GI Forum's founding chapter in Corpus Christi, presented Wanda García with the flag that had draped her late husband's casket. Handing her the flag, Cásares thanked Mrs. García for the sacrifices her husband had made "on behalf of a grateful nation."

Notes

Acknowledgments

[1]   Allsup, Carl. 1982. *The American GI Forum: Origins and Evolution*. University of Texas, Austin: Center for Mexican-American Studies.

[2]   Personal correspondence of Carl Allsup to the author, February 9, 1982.

Introduction

[1]   Croly, Herbert. 1909. *The Promise of American Life*. New York: Macmillan.

[2]   Hofstader, Richard. 1948. *The American Political Tradition*. New York: Vintage Books.

[3]   Morin, Raul. 1963. *Among the Valiant*. California: Borden Publishing Co. See also Meier, Matt S. and Ribera, Feliciano. 1993. *Mexican Americans/American Mexicans: From Conquistadors to Chicanos*. New York: Hill and Wang. 160–161.

[4]   Seventeen Mexican Americans were awarded congressional medals of honor (the nation's highest military service award) for bravery in battle during World War II and Korea, the highest percentage of medal of honor recipients proportionate to the subpopulation represented of any American group.

[5]   Interview with Dr. Hector García, November 1981. See also "Little by Little: Patricia Luna," in Elsasser, Nan, *et al.* 1980. *Las Mujeres: Conversations from a Hispanic Community*, Old Westbury, New York: Feminist Press/McGraw-Hill. 88.

Chapter 1
Veterans and Americans

[1] Morín, Raúl. 1963. *Among the Valiant*. California: Borden Publishing.

[2] *Ibid.* See also Samora, J. and Simon, P. V. 1997. *A History of the Mexican-American People*. London: University of Notre Dame Press. 2.

[3] *Ibid.*

[4] See Camarillo, Albert. 1984. *A History of Mexican-Americans in California*. San Francisco: Boyd & Fraser. 72.

[5] The unusual bravery and valor of Mexican Americans in combat is well documented. In addition to Morin's groundbreaking work *Among the Valiant* and Camarillo's references in *A History of Mexican-Americans in California*, see also Estrada, Leobardo F., *et al.* "Chicanos in the United States: A History of Exploitation and Resistance." In *Latinos in the Political System*, edited by Chris F. García. 1988. Notre Dame: University of Notre Dame Press. 51.

[6] For a more detailed account of delayed benefits to Mexican-American veterans of this era, see Allsup, Carl (hereafter, Allsup). 1982. *The American GI Forum: Origins and Evolution*. University of Texas, Austin: Center for Mexican-American Studies. 33–38.

[7] *The Sentinel* (Corpus Christi), March 26 and April 2, 1948 editions; March 26, 1948 minutes of first American GI Forum meeting, Dr. Hector P. García/American GI Forum Historical Foundation and Archives; Allsup, *supra*, p.34.

[8] Montejano, David. 1987. *Anglos and Mexicans in the Making of Texas, 1836–1986*. Austin: University of Texas Press, citing U. S. Federal Works Agency. 1941. Work Projects Administration Report: *Mexican Migratory Workers of South Texas* (Sheldon C. Merefee, principal investigator). 227.

[9]   Allsup, *supra,* 32.

[10]   See, for example, "President Honors GI Forum Founder," *Nuestro.* (May 1984): 28. The article recounts early efforts by Hector García to hospitalize returning Mexican-American veterans in the Naval Air Station Hospital in Corpus Christi. According to García, "Many of them were very sick—a lot had malaria. So I would try to hospitalize them in the Naval Air Station . . . But they turned us down . . . saying those people are Army . . . and we're Navy . . . I got a little upset . . . and went to various hospitals in Corpus Christi . . . [W]e organized a group of veterans to protest and we were able to get the Veterans Administration to permit the admission of veterans to the Naval Air Station on a contract basis."

[11]   García, Dr. Hector P. and Dr. Clotilde García. November 1981. Interview by author.

[12]   Spanish reference to persons of Mexican origin.

[13].   Hector García interview. 1991. *Supra.*

[14]   No relation to the doctor, Gus García was a constant source of intellectual capital for the Forum during its early years of development. Through his involvement with the organization, he eventually rose to national legal prominence. See, for example, discussion in Chapters 3 and 4 regarding García's particular contributions to Mexican-American efforts to desegregate schools and juries in Texas and other states.

[15]   The GI Forum constitution explicitly stated that the Forum condoned only "the use of non-violent and lawful methods in pursuing the objectives of the organization."

[16]   Outlined in official GI Forum literature, 1948 to present; also, García interview, *supra.*

[17]   *Ibid.*

[18]   Countless women have gained local, state, and national prestige through their involvement with the GI Forum, including Polly Baca Barragán, a former Colorado state senator and vice-chairwoman of

the Democratic National Committee; Sara Barela, a longtime Forum activist who helped to initiate a successful national consumer boycott against the Adolph Coors Brewing Company for its discriminatory employment policies during the late 1960s and 1970s; and Martha Villalobos, four-time National GI Forum Women's chairwoman and a former member of the national board of directors of SER—Jobs for Progress.

[19] Youth members of the early GI Forum years have developed into highly respected leaders both within and outside of the organization. In addition to Polly Baca Barragán and Martha Villalobos (cited above), individuals who have moved on to local, state, and national prominence following experiences in the Junior GI Forum include Raúl Yzaguirre, as president of the National Council of La Raza; Ernest E. García, as deputy special assistant to President Ronald Reagan; and Ed Terrones, as director of the Office of Civil Rights at the U. S. Environmental Protection Agency.

[20] See *Nuestro* (May 1984): 27–31; also case notes provided by Dr. Hector García, November 1981. Allsup, *supra*, 34. One such case was that of Andrés Ramírez, of whom the doctor wrote, "Mr. Ramírez' wife has bled a lot, so Mr. Ramírez brought her to the doctor; the doctor is treating her, can see very clearly that Mr. Ramírez is sicker than his wife. Mr. Ramírez has lost 30 pounds in one year and has malaria. His pension was reduced from $69.00 to $41.00 in December, 1947. Statements were submitted by his doctor as should be done, yet the pension was reduced."

[21] Allsup, *supra*, 35.

[22] *Ibid*, 36.

[23] See *Nuestro* (May 1984): 29, quoting Hector García: "At that time . . . the average Hispanic veteran's education level was perhaps 2.2 years of school, which was fantastic illiteracy . . . A lot of them didn't have a job . . . so we started setting up schools in conjunction with the Veterans Administration and the local school system." The idea, according to García, was to confront the problems of illiteracy and joblessness head-on with schooling and job training directed to those who needed them most.

[24] *Ibid.*

[25] These drives were sponsored to encourage exercise of Mexican-American rights and access to public institutions, which were frequently discouraged for *mexicanos* by Anglo citizens and officials. The Forum and other Mexican-American groups opposed the poll tax of $1.75 then levied, arguing that it discouraged many Mexican Americans from voting. But until Forum and other civil rights activists were able to secure the elimination of the tax in the mid-1960s, they used drives to maximize the Mexican-American voting franchise. (See Chapter 4 for further discussion.)

[26] Interviews with Dr. Hector García and Rosa Ena Gutiérrez, November 1981. See also *Nuestro* (May 1984): 29.

[27] Allsup, *supra*, 40.

[28] *Ibid*, 41.

[29] Notarized statements of George Groh and Hector García, February 1949, GI Forum Historical Foundation and Archives.

[30] Letter of Dr. Hector García to Senator Lyndon B. Johnson, January 10, 1949, *ibid.*

[31] "Funeral Home Action Draws Forum Protest." *Corpus Christi Caller-Times.* 11 January 1949. Also "Latin Service Discouraged by Rice Funeral Home." *Caller-Times.* 11 January 1949.

[32] Rogers Kelley to Dr. García via telegram, January 1949, GI Forum Historical Foundation and Archives.

[33] Texas Governor Beauford Jester to Dr. García via telegram, January 11, 1949, *ibid.*

[34] Oscar Phillips' *Reader's Digest* article on Dr. Hector García, GI Forum Historical Foundation and Archives; Allsup, *supra*, 42.

[35] Lyndon B. Johnson to Dr. García via telegram, January 11, 1949.

[36] Hector García interview. 1991. *Supra.*

[37] *Three Rivers News*. 1949. Editorial, 20 January.

[38] Resolution of American Legion Post 121, Waco, Texas, January 12, 1949, GI Forum Historical Foundation and Archives.

[39] Allsup, *supra*, 45.

[40] *Ibid*, 46.

[41] *Ibid*.

[42] *Ibid*.

[43] Notarized statement of George Groh, February 1949, and testimony, April 1949, GI Forum Historical Foundation and Archives.

[44] Allsup, *supra*, 47. According to Allsup, several attempts were made by the president of the Three Rivers Chamber of Commerce, the mayor, and the city secretary to secure Guadalupe Longoria's signature on a statement denouncing the Forum and its involvement in the Longoria affair.

[45] *Ibid*.

[46] *Ibid*, 48.

[47] Rogers Kelley quoted in *Corpus Christi Caller-Times*. 8 April 1949. GI Forum Historical Foundation and Archives.

[48] Minority Report of House Committee, H.S.R. 68, April 7, 1949, GI Historical Foundation and Archives.

[49] "Rep. Tinsley Asks Report on Longoria Case Be Withdrawn." *Corpus Christi Caller-Times*. April 1949. GI Forum Historical Foundation and Archives.

Chapter 2
Building from the Ground Up

[1]   See Díaz de Cossió, Roger, *et al.* 1997. *Los mexicanos en Estados. Sistemas Técnicos de Edición.* Mexico City: S.A. de C.V. 157–158.

[2]   See Gúzman, Ralph C. 1976. *The Political Socialization of the Mexican-American People.* New York: Arno Press. 137–143.

[3]   See Menchaca, Martha. 1995. *The Mexican Outsiders.* Austin: University of Texas Press. 105.

[4]   Ximenes, Vicente. December 1981. Interview by author.

[5]   Yzaguirre, Raúl. December 1981. Interview by author.

[6]   Particularly relevant are the *Delgado* and *Hernández* cases discussed in Chapters 3 and 4.

[7]   Leininger Pycior, Julie. 1997. *LBJ and Mexican-Americans.* Austin: University of Texas. 60.

[8]   Ferber, Edna. 1952. *Giant.* Garden City, New York: Doubleday; also García interview, *supra.*

[9]   Akers, Cecilia. March 10, 1998. Interview by author.

[10]   Téllez, Louis. November 1981. Interview by author; and Ximenes interview, *supra.*

[11]   *Ibid.*

[12]   While issues of male-female conflict in the GI Forum and the general topic of Latina feminism are not considered here, interested readers may consult Orozco, Cynthia E. 1995. "Beyond Machismo, La Familia, and Ladies Auxiliaries." *Perspectives in Mexican-American Studies.* (5): 3–34. Tucson: University of Arizona; Bonilla-Santiago, Gloria. 1992. *Breaking Ground and Barriers*: *Hispanic Women Developing Effective Leadership.* San Diego: Marin Publications. 74; Melville, Margarita B. 1980. *Twice A Minority: Mexican-American*

Women. St. Louis: C. V. Mosby. 226–227; and Enriquez, Evangelina and Mirandé, Alfredo. 1979. *La Chicana: The Mexican-American Women*. Chicago: University of Chicago. 1981.

[13]   *Tamaladas* is a *mexicano* reference to sales of tamales.

[14]   Memorandum from Isabelle Téllez to the author, July 1982.

[15]   American GI Forum Women of the United States. 1980 Calendar, SER-Jobs for Progress Women's Division, Dallas, Texas.

[16]   Coronado, Dominga. July 1982. Interview by author.

[17]   *Ibid.* See also, Gómez-Quiñones, Juan. 1990. *Chicano Politics: Reality and Promise, 1940–1990*. Albuquerque: University of New Mexico. 61.

[18]   See Cotera, Marta (undated; *circa* 1974): 98. *Profile on the Mexican-American Woman.* Austin: National Educational Laboratory Publishers, Inc.

[19]   During this period, Louis Téllez served as the national GI Forum secretary.

[20]   A more detailed discussion of the school desegregation movement is included in Chapter 3.

[21]   American GI Forum Women of the United States. Calendar, 1980, *supra*; also Isabelle Téllez papers.

[22]   Official GI Forum Organizational Chart.

[23]   *Ibid.* For supporting reference to the Forum's national membership base, see also Gómez- Quiñones, *supra,* 175.

[24]   Official GI Forum organizational records.

[25]   See, for example, "Reagan, Hispanics Schedule Secret Meeting in El Paso." 1983. *El Paso Herald-Post.* 12 August, A1 and A4.

Chapter 3
Education Reform

[1]   See Haro, Carlos M. 1977, 1. *Mexicano/Chicano Concerns and School Desegregation in Los Angeles*. Monograph 9. University of California, Los Angeles: Chicano Studies Center Publications. According to Haro, "Only in one state, New Mexico, did the Spanish surname group have a higher school completion average, 0.3 years, than the black. Still, that group was 4.8 years lower than the Anglo group."

[2]   Hector García interview, 1981, *supra;* see also, García, Mario T. 1994. *Memories of Chicano History: The Life and Narrative of Bert Corona*, Berkeley/Los Angeles: University of California Press. 44–55.

[3]   See, e.g., Pinchot, Jane. 1989. *The Mexicans in America*. Minneapolis: Lerner Publications. 56.

[4]   *Ibid.* See also, Marquez, Benjamin. 1993. *LULAC: The Evolution of a Mexican-American Political Organization*. Austin: University of Texas Press. 51–53.

[5]   Moore, Joan W. 1970. *Mexican-Americans*. New Jersey: Prentice Hall. 78.

[6]   Alcalá, Carlos M. and Rangel, Jorge C. 1972. "Chicanos in Texas Schools." *Harvard Civil Rights and Civil Liberties Law Review*. 7(2): 307. (Hereafter Alcalá and Rangel.)

[7]   *Independent School District v. Salvatierra*, 33 S. W. 2d 790 (1930).

[8]   According to Montejano (1987, 285–286), Ozona, Texas history offers a striking example of the "stubborn and uneven nature of Jim Crow for Mexicans . . . In this town, drugstores were closed to Mexican-Americans until the late 1940s. Restaurants and movie houses did not open to Mexican-Americans until the early 1950s; hotels were exclusively reserved for Anglo patrons until about 1958; barber and beauty shops were segregated until 1969; and until the early 1970s, the bowling alley, cemeteries, and swimming pools still remained segregated."

[9] Cited in Garza, Edward. 1951. "LULAC: League of United Latin American citizens." MA: Southwest Texas State Teachers College.

[10] In 1947, for example, three University of Texas student groups (including Ed Idar's Laredo Club and Cris Alderete's Alba Club) issued a press release outlining and denouncing the segregationist policies of the Beeville, Sinton, Elgin, Bastrop, and Cotulla school districts. The superintendents of the respective schools defended their policies with support from the Texas State Department of Education [see e.g., Leff, Gladys R. December 1976. "George I. Sánchez: Don Quixote of the Southwest." Doctoral dissertation. Denton: North Texas State University (hereafter Leff), citing interview with Ed Idar, Jr. July 31, 1973, 412. See also Alcalá and Rangel, and Allsup, *supra*]. "Educational opportunities offered Latin Americans are equal to those offered Anglo Americans," claimed the superintendents of the Beeville and Sinton schools in a joint prepared statement. The statement went on to conclude: "As soon as language deficiencies are overcome, it is the desire and policy of both schools to move the [Mexican-Americans] into classrooms with Anglo Americans." [*Ibid.* Quote cited in Allsup from Corpus Christi *Caller-Times,* "2 School Heads Admit Charges of Segregation." October 1947. 83 n. 14.] Technically correct as the statement may have been, the reality was that Mexican-American students were typically separated from Anglo students through the eighth grade in these schools.

[11] *Méndez v. Westminster,* 67 F. Supp. 544 (S. D. Cal. 1946), aff'd 161 F. 2d 774 (9th cir. 1947).

[12] *Ibid.* at 780. The exceptions included "Indians under certain circumstances and children of Chinese, Japanese or Mongolian parentage."

[13] *Ibid.* See also Alcalá and Rangel 1972, 336, for an excellent account of the *Méndez* case. According to Alcalá and Rangel: "The court did not hold that segregation of Mexican-American children violated the Fourteenth Amendment *per se.* On the contrary, California could pass a law to segregate Mexican-American children. But absent such a law, Chicano segregation was unconstitutional."

[14] Sánchez, George I. and Strickland, V.E. 1947. *Study of the Educational Opportunities Provided Spanish-Surname Children in the*

Texas School Systems. Austin: University of Texas, citing letter from Gus García to Price Daniel, dated August 18, 1947.

[15]   *Ibid.,* citing letter response from Price Daniel to Gus García, dated August 21, 1947.

[16]   *Ibid.* Also Hector García interview 1981.

[17]   *Ibid.*

[18]   *Delgado v. Bastrop Independent School District,* Civil No. 388 (W. D. Tex., June 15, 1948).

[19]   In Corpus Christi, Hector García immediately took up support of the *Delgado* case, raising $2,000 in three months through a LULAC committee he headed to assist the efforts of Gus García and the various families involved in the legal challenge to local and state authorities. García's efforts on behalf of *Delgado* were heightened after the GI Forum was established in March 1948. Under Dr. García's leadership the Forum quickly solicited additional financial and material support for participating families and for general publicity related to the case. Hector García interview 1981.

[20]   Civil No. 388 (W. D. Tex., June 15, 1948).

[21]   *Ibid.* See also Alcalá and Rangel 1972, 337 n. 175.

[22]   Alcalá and Rangel, 1972, 337, citing Texas State Department of Education. 1948–49. *Standards and Activities of the Division of Supervision and Accreditation of School Systems.* Bulletin 507.

[23]   Civil No. 388 (W. D. Tex., June 15, 1948). See also Alcalá and Rangel, 1972, 337. In the *Delgado* ruling Judge Rice permitted the defendant school districts, and so by inference all Texas districts, to maintain separate classes on the same campus and in the first grade "solely for instructional purposes" as determined by "scientific and standardized tests" equally administered and applied to all pupils in regard to their understanding and competency in the English language.

[24]   *Ibid.* Following the judge's June 15, 1948 ruling, the districts were given until September of 1949 to comply. Note Appendix I, Civil No. 388 (W. D. Tex., June 15, 1948).

[25]   Hector García interview 1981. Also note *Mathis* and *Driscoll* cases cited later in this chapter.

[26]   *Ibid.* Del Rio, a particularly obstinant district, had been the defendant in *Independent School District v. Salvatierra*, 33 S. W. 2d 790 (Tex. Civ. App., 4th Dt., 1930). See also Allsup 1982, 121.

[27]   It is important to note that Forum members and many in the Mexican-American community at large were highly prone to favor progressive integration of *all* races in the public schools. One Forum survey in 1955, for example, showed that 77 percent surveyed supported integration of blacks, versus only 62 percent of blacks themselves. "Mexican-Americans Favor Negro School Integration." 1955. *GI Forum News Bulletin.* Sept.–Oct.

[28]   Allsup 1982, 90. Allsup's description of conditions in the Sandia, Texas school district at the time, for example, speaks to the point of white advantage: "The Sandia school system consisted of a Mexican ward school and an Anglo school. While the main Anglo school building was a two story brick building with a good playground, the Mexican classes were held in a frame building that by 1952 was no more that a shack with poor ventilation and improper heat; the playground was a field with several craters. *Mexicano* elementary classes through third grade had twenty-five students and one teacher, whereas the corresponding ratio for the Anglo school was ten to one."

[29]   Alcalá and Rangel 1972, 338. The superintendent's report recommended that accreditation be withheld because students were segregated and Latin American teachers were "unacceptable" in the Anglo school. The report further indicated that "elementary children of the two races were, by board regulation, not permitted to mix."

[30]   State Board of Education—Members Act, General and Special Laws, Texas Ch. 546, paragraph 12 (1949).

[31] Public Free Schools Administration Act, Ch. 299, Art. V., Texas Laws (1949), as amended Tex. Educ. Code, Paragraphs 11.25, 11.51, and 11.52 (Vernon Supp. 1971).

[32] Alcalá and Rangel 1972, 339. See also *The Daily Texan*. 1949. Austin. 1 March.

[33] "Resolution of the American GI Forum of Texas, State Convention 1949, on Federal Aid to Education and Segregation," September 26, 1949, GI Forum Historical Foundation and Archives; Allsup 1982, 87.

[34] Spanish term for neighborhoods used in the Chicano vernacular to connote *mexicano* neighborhoods and communities.

[35] Hector García interview 1981.

[36] Texas Education Agency (TEA). 1950. *Statement of Policy Pertaining to Segregation of Latin American Children.* May 8. See also Allsup 1982, 88, citing June 21, 1950 letter of J. D. Edgar to county school superintendents, interpreting TEA's policy statement.

[37] This is not to say that some efforts did not succeed. Forum attorneys persuaded state officials to order corrective action in important state board appeals concerning the Sanderson and Hondo school districts. See Allsup 1982, 90–91. Unfortunately, even in those cases where Forum attorneys prevailed in the state review process, their victories were somewhat empty. First, successful decisions were exceptional and suspiciously difficult to come by. Second, and more importantly, they were easily and consistently ignored by local school officials.

[38] "Forum Committee Visits Carrizo Springs, Reports No Sign of Segregation." *Forum News Bulletin*. March 1956.

[39] "Kingsville Segregation Settled, But No Thanks To Commissioner Edgar." *Forum News Bulletin*. Sept.–Oct. 1955.

[40] Edgar testimony from Civil Action No. 1385, Motion to Dismiss by Defendants, December 21, 1955, GI Forum Historical Foundation and Archives.

[41]   Dismissal resulted from refusal of the case's expert witness to testify. Forum attorneys did not pursue the suit because at the time there was no requirement for balancing and no law on tracking. See Alcalá and Rangel 1972, 345 n. 228.

[42]   TEA Action: *Guerrero v. Mathis Independent School District,* decided by commissioner Edgar May 11, 1955.

[43]   *Hernandez v. Driscoll Consolidated Independent School District,* S.D. Tex., January 11, 1957. See also Loya, Anamaría C. 1990. "Chicanos, Law, and Educational Reform." *La Raza Law Journal.* Berkeley: University of California. 3 (Spring): 36 and Romo, Ricardo. 1986. "George I. Sánchez and the Civil Rights Movement: 1940-1960." *La Raza Law Journal,* Berkeley: University of California. 1 (Fall): 358-359.

[44]   *Hernandez v. Driscoll Consolidated Independent School District,* S.D. Tex., January 11, 1957.

[45]   *U.S. v. Texas,* 342 F. Supp. 27–28, E. D. Tex. (1971).

[46]   Alcalá and Rangel 1972, 319–320.

[47]   *The Excluded Student; Educational Practices Affecting Mexican-Americans in the Southwest Politics: Reality and Promise, 1940–1990,* 1990. Albuquerque: University of New Mexico. 87.

Chapter 4
Early Struggles for Justice and Equal Opportunity

[1]   Acuña, Rodolfo. 1988. *Occupied America.* New York: HarperCollins (hereafter, Acuña). 254–256. Acuña reports that the grand jury investigation in the Sleepy Lagoon case was significantly informed by Captain Ed Ayres of the Los Angeles Police Department's Foreign Relations Bureau. Citing a work by the poet and fiction writer Rudyard Kipling, Ayres argued that the "Mexican was an Indian, that the Indian was an Oriental, and that the Oriental had an utter disregard for life. Therefore, since the Chicano was an Oriental and had this inborn characteristic, he was consequently violent. Furthermore, the

Chicano was cruel, for he was a descendant of the Aztecs, who allegedly sacrificed 30,000 victims a day."

[2] *Ibid.,* 256. The defendants were not exonerated until October 4, 1944, when the California District Court of Appeals unanimously reversed the lower court's convictions and dismissed all charges for lack of evidence.

[3] Montejano, David. 1987. *Anglos and Mexicans in the Making of Texas, 1836–1986.* Austin: University of Texas Press. 229.

[4] The Bracero Program was established in 1943 through an international agreement between the United States and Mexico. Many Chicano academics today challenge the notion that foreign workers were actually necessary to import for agricultural production. After the Bracero Program's extension following the war, GI Forum leaders frequently documented areas where domestic labor was available and willing to perform in positions held by cheaper and more exploitable Mexican labor. For an especially excellent critique of the Bracero Program, see Calavita, Kitty. 1992. *Inside the State: The Bracero Program, Immigration and the INS.* New York: Routledge.

[5] *Braceros* were Mexican laborers brought to the United States to fill jobs under the Bracero Program.

[6] *Ibid,* 32. Later, at 35, Calavita reports that by June 1950, it was estimated that as many as 50,000 illegal aliens were crowded into the lower Rio Grande Valley alone.

[7] Rasmussen, Wayne D. 1951. *A History of the Emergency Farm Labor Supply Program, 1943–1947.* Washington, D. C.: U. S. Department of Agriculture, Bureau of Agricultural Economics. Agricultural Monograph, No. 13 (cited in Calavita 1992, 24).

[8] McWilliams, Carey. 1949. "California and the Wetback." *Common Ground.* Summer.

[9] *Ibid.* Acuña states that U. S. newspapers significantly supported the exclusion of foreign workers and aroused anti-alien sentiments during the McCarthy era, portraying undocumented workers as dangerous, malicious, and subversive.

[10]   García, Mario T. 1994. *Memories of Chicano History: The Life and Narrative of Bert Corona*. Berkeley/Los Angeles: University of California. 184.

[11]   See, for example, Grebler, Leo, *et al.* 1970. *The Mexican-American People*. New York: Free Press. 521–522 (hereafter Grebler).

[12]   Yzaguirre, Raúl. December 1981. Interview by author.

[13]   Ximenes, Vicente. December 1981. Interview by author.

[14]   García, Hector. November 1981. Interview by author.

[15]   Allsup, Carl 1992, 102–103.

[16]   *Ibid.*, 107; "Report on Wetback Problem." December 1953. *Forum News Bulletin*. Published by Forum/AFL; and May 1954. *Stanford Law Review*. (The *Law Review* article cited *What Price Wetbacks* as an authoritative source.)

[17]   *Ibid.*, 266. According to Acuña, approximately 8 percent of United States cotton was machine-harvested in 1950, for example. By 1964, the final year of *bracero* contracting, the figure had risen to 78 percent. In California and Arizona, two leading *bracero* states, 97 percent of the 1964 cotton crop was machine-harvested.

[18]   "Welfare Payments Light Among Agricultural Workers." January 1956 *Forum News Bulletin*; Vicente Ximenes interview 1981.

[19]   *Pete Hernández, Petitioner v. State of Texas*, 347 U.S. 475 (1954).

[20]   "Railroad Unions Being Scrutinized by FEPC." October 1956. *Forum News Bulletin*; see also, Allsup 1982, 100.

[21]   *Ibid.*, "Sen. Chávez Enters Railway Brotherhood Clause Tiff." November 1956 and "New Mexico Forums Win . . ." January 1958.

[22]   *Ibid.*, 100; "DAR's Patriotic Work in Colorado Vindicated." 1957. *Corpus Christi Caller-Times*. 18 February; Hector García interview 1981.

[23] Hector García interview 1981.

[24] Allsup 1982, 70; "Poll Tax Drive in Valley." November 1956. *Forum News Bulletin.*

[25] See Montejano 1987, 279. According to Montejano, "Anglo-Texans reacted in fashion typical of the times by calling these efforts 'Communist-inspired.' The veterans organizations, however, were able to withstand the 'fifth columnist' slander commonly used against activists."

[26] *Ibid.,* 1955. *Corpus Christi Caller-Times,* 22 December; 1956. *Brownsville Herald,* 25 January.

[27] "Poll Tax Drive in Valley." 1956. *Forum News Bulletin.* November.

[28] Yzaguirre presentation on "The Evolution of Chicano/Hispanic Organizations and Politics," at Georgetown University, Washington, D. C., March 1981.

Chapter 5
The Kennedy and Johnson Years

[1] Salinger, Pierre. 1966. *With Kennedy.* New York: Doubleday. 29.

[2] Kennedy, John F. 1964. *A Nation of Immigrants.* New York: Harper & Row. See "Introduction," by Robert F. Kennedy, ix.

[3] American GI Forum Constitution, Article II, Sec. 4.

[4] "Kennedy Joins GI Forum." 1960. *Forum News,* June.

[5] "Demos Pledge Aid . . ." 1960. *Forum News,* September. Hector García interview 1981; Allsup 1982, 131.

[6] Hector García interview 1981. JFK expressed his gratitude to García in the White House in 1961. According to García:

At the conclusion of our meeting, Kennedy said, "Dr. García, I want you to know that I am very grateful to the Mexican-American people." He took me aside to take a picture and when the shot was taken he said, "I want you to show this picture to all of the Mexican-American people and thank them for having elected me president of the United States."

Later, reflecting back on the event, García assessed the president's actions and their ultimate significance:

Kennedy recognized our potential and after that it was easy selling the concept of Mexican-American voter clubs because every politician in the world now wanted our votes.

[7]   Allsup 1982, 189 n.12, notes Robert Kennedy's remarks from the *Kansas City Star*, "Mexicans Pleased by Election of Kennedy," November 1960. The voting differentials cited for Illinois and Texas are from Miller, Merle. 1980. *Lyndon*. New York: Ballantine. 333.

[8]   Leff, Gladys. 1976. "George I. Sánchez: Don Quixote of the Southwest." Doctoral dissertation. Denton: North Texas State University. 450; Hector García interview 1981.

[9]   Kearns, Doris. 1976. *Lyndon Johnson and the American Dream*. New York: Harper & Row. 210-213.

[10]   Miller, Merle, *Lyndon*. Quote of D. B. Hardeman on Johnson and the Felix Longoria incident at Three Rivers, 175. In a November 1981 interview with the author, Hector García agreed with Miller's assessment. According to García,"No one can make the accusation that Johnson helped us to gain political power . . . because we had no political power at the time. We were just getting started and we didn't have any votes." In García's assessment, Johnson helped the Forum's cause because it was the right thing to do in his judgement.

[11]   See Leininger Pycior, *supra,* 73-76 and 105 for Johnson's efforts to appeal to interests against the Forum's counsel on issues ranging from farm labor policy to police brutality.

[12]   See García, F. Chris. 1988. *Latinos and the Political System*. Notre Dame: University of Notre Dame Press. 501. The impacts of Latino inclusion under the Voting Rights Act's extension and amendment of

Congress in 1975 have been profound. According to Chicano scholar F. Chris García, for example, "California Hispanic registration . . . increased from 715,600 in 1976 to 988,130 in 1980 and 1,136,497 in 1984. In Texas the Hispanic registration rate climed from 32 percent in 1976 to 51 percent in 1984. Across the nation from 1972 to 1984, Latino registration increased 27 percent compared to . . . a 9 percent increase in white voters."

[13]   García, Mario T. 1994. *Memories of Chicano History: The Life and Narrative of Bert Corona.* Berkeley: University of California Press. 220.

[14]   Huelga. 1966. *Forumeer.* April. 1. For excellent assessments of the strike's background and the issues involved, see Meister, Dick and Loftis, Anne. 1977. *A Long Time Coming: The Struggle to Unionize America's Farm Workers.* New York: Macmillan; see also Allen, Steve. 1966. *The Ground is Our Table.* New York: Doubleday.

[15]   *Ibid.*

[16]   *Ibid.*

[17]   *Forumeer.* Editorial. April 1966; Hector García interview 1981.

[18]   "Forum Delegates Walk Out." *Forumeer.* April 1966.

[19]   "EEOC Charged—Discrimination." *Forumeer.* June 1966.

[20]   *Ibid.;* Yzaguirre interview 1981; see also, Califano, Joseph A., Jr. 1991.*The Triumph and Tragedy of Lyndon Johnson: The White House Years,* Simon & Schuster. 135-136.

[21]   See Acuña 1982, 341.

[22]   *Ibid.,* Acuña offers excellent background sketches on Gonzáles, Gutiérrez, and Tijerina, 338-342. For background on Corona, see García, Mario T. 1994.

[23]   Barragán, Polly Baca. December 1981. Interview with author.

[24] Ximenes interview 1981. "SER Funded—$5,000,000." *Forumeer.* June 1967.

[25] The meeting with the Mexican president involved a treaty signing to cede Mexico-disputed lands along the U.S.-Mexico border.

[26] Baca Barragán interview 1981.

[27] Ximenes interview 1981. Apparently, a "national security threat" was determined to exist on the basis of there being multiple cabinet participants at the hearings along with the president and vice-president, the suggestion being that any harm to participating administration officials, through violence or conspiracy, could create problems of executive succession and government decision-making authority.

[28] Baca Barragán interview 1981; see also Acuña 1982, 341 for a more detailed account of Tijerina's courthouse raid.

[29] Téllez, Louis. November 1981. Interview with author.

[30] See García, 225–227. The gathering was attended by nearly 1,200 protesters. The protesters called themselves La Raza Unida, a third-party movement in Texas.

[31] See, e.g., "1,000 at M-A Hearings in El Paso." 1967. *Forumeer.* November. 1.

[32] "President Reports Actions to Aid Spanish-speaking Citizens." White House Press Release. January 1968.

[33] *Ibid.;* and Vicente Ximenes, "Keynote Address," 20th Annual National GI Forum Convention, August 8, 1968.

[34] John Gardner interview, 1994. According to Gardner, "Johnson probably had a far more natural understanding of Mexican-Americans than of blacks or any other minority population and it was widely known in the administration that he had an especially friendly attitude towards Mexican-Americans." See also, *Nuestro*, May 1984, 31, which includes the following quote from Hector García, "It was Lyndon Johnson . . . who opened the door, on a man-to-man basis, or a woman-to-woman basis, a people-to-people basis, really, for

Mexican-Americans and Hispanics in the United States, making it possible to improve conditions. Why? He didn't have to do it. It was because he wanted things done and he liked people. He liked us."

Chapter 6
Economic and Employment Struggles

[1]   Vogel, David. 1977. *Lobbying the Corporation.* New York: Basic Books. 3 and 7.

[2]   The Los Angeles-based United Neighborhoods Organization (UNO) was a major force in challenging insurance red-lining discrimination in East Los Angeles. Hispanic community protests regarding foundation expenditures and policies were well-founded; when Vicente Ximenes called a special White House meeting to discuss foundation giving to Hispanics in 1968, only two of fifty foundations invited responded. Vicente Ximenes interview 1981.

[3]   National Council of La Raza. "Out of the Picture: Hispanics and the Media," in Rodríguez, Clara E., ed. 1997. *Latin Looks: Images of Latinos and Latinas in the U. S. Media.* Westview Press. 21-35.

[4]   Ximenes interview, Ximenes White House correspondence to Steck-Vaughn, April 1969; "Forum Protests Insulting Ad." 1969. *Forumeer.* October.

[5]   "Coors Boycott On." 1969. *Forumeer.* April.

[6]   "Summary of Convention Resolutions." 1968. *Forumeer.* August.

[7]   "Coors Boycott On." 1969. *Forumeer.* April.

[8]   "Coors Guilty of Discrimination." 1970. *Forumeer.* September.

[9]   Téllez, Louis. November 1981; Vicente Ximenes; Polly Baca Barragán, December 1981; Raul Yzaguirre, December 1981. Interviews with author. "Coors Guilty . . ." 1970. *Forumeer.* September.

[10] Alarid, Jake. April 1998. Los Angeles. Interview with author.

[11] "SER-Jobs For Progress." Annual Report. 1979. *Partners With Business*. 2 (hereafter: SER Annual-'79). "Project SER Office Open." 1966. *Forumeer*. November.

[12] "SER Funded . . ." 1967. *Forumeer*. June.

[13] García, Dr. Clotilde. November 1981. Interview with author.

[14] Martínez, Carlos. August 1994. Interview with author.

[15] "VOP . . . Did the Job." 1974. *Forumeer*. May; Allsup 1982, 147.

Chapter 7
The "Decade of the Hispanic" and the New Federalism

[1] "It's Your Turn in the Sun." 1978. *Time*. October 16: 48.

[2] Among others, *Newsweek, U. S. News and World Report, The New York Times*, and the *Washington Post* ran feature reports on Hispanic Americans in 1980–1981.

[3] López was especially commented on for scrawling on his prison wall, while captive in Iran: *"Que viva el rojo, blanco y azul!"* (Long live the red, white and blue!)

[4] Carter's early appointments included Hispanics to head or sub-stantively represent the Immigration and Naturalization Service, and the Departments of Housing and Urban Development, Health, Education and Welfare, and Interior. Carter also made several key Hispanic appointments to the federal judiciary, including GI Forum legal adviser James De Anda. See de la Garza, Rodolfo O. "Chicano Elites and National Policymaking, 1977-80: Passive or Active Representatives." in García, F. Chris. 314–327.

[5]   See Acuña 1982, 385.

[6]   See Schieffer 1989, 16.

[7]   During my association with Cano as his special assistant and adviser, during 1981-1983, I observed first-hand (and tried to mitigate) the ire he could provoke in friends and enemies alike. The tendency was always matched by a genuine and endearing commitment to public purposes; and those who best knew Cano understood this. Raúl Yzaguirre, one of Cano's closest friends, said in delivering the eulogy at his funeral in 1988, "In the heat of battle, under the pressure of deadlines, and in the storm of controversy, José could, and often would, exhibit his all-too-human and earthly frailties. He was human enough to lose his temper, earthy enough to spice his language with a few expletives. But it was a righteous anger, a purposeful irritation . . . it was the intolerance of one who desperately wanted to get things done . . . and it was easy to forgive."

[8]   In fact, an uneasy balance between organizational support for the New Federalism's promise of new jobs and income, and opposition to those aspects of Reagan's policies that hit at minority interests would mark Forum strategy throughout the early Reagan presidency.

[9]   Cano, José R. 1981. "Hispanic America in the Era of New Republicanism." *Forumeer.* January. 1.

[10]   Western Union Mailgram from José R. Cano to Edwin Meese. December 31, 1981.

[11]   Correspondence to President Ronald Reagan. February 13, 1981. José Cano Papers.

[12]   Correspondence of national Hispanic organizational leaders to President Ronald W. Reagan. 1981 (sent via National Council of La Raza president Raúl Yzaguirre). January 7. 1.

[13]   "Fight Back: Hispanics May Change Tactics." 1981. *The Saginaw News.* 22 March.

[14]   Other attending Latino leaders included Hector Barreto, National Hispanic Chamber of Commerce; Raúl Yzaguirre, National Council of La Raza; Manuel Bustelo, National Puerto Rican Forum; Pedro Garza, SER; Guarione Díaz, Cuban National Planning Council; and Wilma Espinosa, Mexican-American Women's National Association.

[15]   "Chairman Cano Visits Reagan and Other Administration Officials in Washington." 1981. *Forumeer*. March. 1.

[16]   Olivera, Mercedes. 1981. "Warning Issued on Bilingual Decision." *Dallas Morning News*. 5 February.

[17]   GI Forum press release. 1981. "Cano Visits Reagan, López Portillo at White House." June 9. 1.

[18]   Testimony of American GI Forum National Chairman José R. Cano before the United States Senate Labor and Human Resources Committee. July 29, 1981.

[19]   *Ibid.,* 4. According to Cano, "Too often, under the current program, the incentive for employers to emphasize minority and female hiring and upward mobility is broken down even further by way of the Office of Federal Contract Compliance's misguided assumption of sanctioning powers. Processing of individual complaints of alleged employer discrimination, even where there are class implications, does not coincide with the overall mission of the Office . . . This responsibility falls more logically within the purview of the Equal Employment Opportunity Commission (EEOC). Still, OFCCP continues to operate within the realm of processing complaints of employment discrimination. This results not only in a duplication of tasks *vis-a-vis* the EEOC, but also in an unnecessary expenditure of resources, which otherwise could be used more constructively towards realizing the intended ends of executive order 11246."

[20]   Torres made these remarks to me, in my capacity as Cano's special assistant for business and government relations.

[21] Remarks of Dr. Hector P. García. 1981. To the American GI Forum Members, Officers and Families at the Annual Convention—Dallas, Texas. American GI Forum 1981 Annual National Convention Brochure. A Hispanic Salute to America. Dallas. 2.

[22] Press release. 1981. "Remarks of José R. Cano, National GI Forum . . . Press Conference . . ." 6 August. North Park Inn, Dallas.

[23] See Acuña 1982, 382. According to Acuña (citing the *Los Angeles Times*, October 2, 1985 edition), 21.5 percent of all U.S. Latinos were legally impoverished in 1972. In 1982, that figure was 29.6 percent.

[24] CETA's Republican-sponsored replacement, for example, the Job Training Partnership Act (JTPA) and the Economic Development Administration (EDA).

[25] The Forum's opposition to including bilingual education in block-grant funding to states and localities was most effectively joined by the Congressional Hispanic Caucus and the National Council of La Raza. According to Acuña 1982, 387, the Reagan budgets between 1981 and 1984 permitted significant (38 percent) reductions in bilingual education funding. The reductions could have been far greater without the Forum's intervention.

[26] Martínez, Carlos. August 1994. Interview with author.

[27] National Chairman's Report. 1981. Annual Report of José R. Cano to the American GI Forum National Membership. August. 8.

[28] "Reagan, Hispanics Schedule Secret Meeting in El Paso." 1983. *El Paso Herald-Post*, 12 August. A1.

[29] "Democrat Blasts Group's Leaders." 1983. *El Paso Herald-Post*. 11 August. A1.

[30] "White Blasts Reagan's Policies." 1983. *El Paso Herald-Post*. 11 August. A1-2.

[31]   "Reagan, Hispanics . . ." 1983, A4.

[32]   Summary of August 12, 1983 Meeting between President Ronald Reagan and Hispanic Community Leaders: Marriott Hotel, El Paso. Memorandum from the author to José R. Cano. August 1983.

[33]   "Reagan Vows to Stand by Latinos." 1983. *Los Angeles Times*. 13 August. A1 and A30.

[34]   This is a recollection of the author, who participated at the meeting with Reagan, *et al*. The exchange between Velásquez and Dr. García was spurred by a question I asked Velásquez following the presidential meeting.

[35]   After praising García's many contributions to the Forum's development, Reagan announced that he would soon be making public a very special honor, to be bestowed upon García, which he was not yet at liberty to share publicly. In March of the following year, on the Forum's 36th anniversary, García was awarded the distinguished Presidential Medal of Freedom for meritorious public service. Reagan personally awarded the medal to García at a special White House ceremony. The Medal of Freedom is the highest honor a U. S. president can bestow upon a civilian. It is awarded to Americans who have distinguished themselves in either public service or the arts and sciences.

[36]   "Special Interest Politics Decried in Reagan Speech to Hispanics." 1983. *Oakland Tribune* (from *Washington Post, New York Times* and AP dispatches). 13 August.

[37]   Remarks of José Cano to the author, August 1983.

[38]   Even Reagan's contemporaneous reductions in national bilingual education funding should not detract from the significance of his recognition of the policy as a political reality.

Chapter 8
Summing Up

[1]   See, e.g., Gomez-Quinones, 181.

[2]   See, e.g., "GI Forum Opens New Plant," *La Prensa* (San Antonio), July 1997; also "Texas: Employment Ahead," *The Stars and Stripes* (Washington, D. C.), July 29, 1997.

[3]   See, e.g., "Testimony on Hispanic Veterans Before the [U. S. House] Sub-Committee on Oversight and Investigations by Jake Alarid, National Commander, American GI Forum of the U. S.," September 28, 1994.

[4]   HACR is the nation's leading corporate responsibility group focused on Latino community issues. Participating HACR organizations include the American GI Forum, the Cuban American National Planning Committee, the National Council of La Raza, the National Puerto Rican Coalition, and the U. S. Hispanic Chamber of Commerce. The Greenlining Institute is a San Francisco-based coalition focused on finance industry accountability to minority and low-income consumers.

[5]   See Acuña 1982, 380; "National Agreement between Adolph Coors Company and a Coalition of Hispanic Organizations," October 29, 1984; Jake Alarid interview, October 1994.

[6]   Meier & Ribera, 253 and 203.

[7]   Estrada, Leobardo F., *et al.*, "Chicanos in the United States: A History of Exploitation and Resistance" in *Latinos and the Political System*, Garcia, F. Chris, ed., University of Notre Dame Press, Notre Dame, 1988, 52.

Epilogue

[1]   McCormack, John. 1996. "Garcia, Hispanic Giant in Civil Rights, Dies at 84." *San Antonio Express-News*. 27 July. 1A.

[2]   Riojas Esparza, Alma. 1996. "AGIF's Breakthroughs in Washington." *The National Forumeer*. San Marcos, TX, August, 3, and Llanas, Raul S. 1996. "Hero Is Gone . . ." *La Prensa*. San Antonio. 31 July. 1.

[3]   Perez, Toni. 1996. "GI Forum Bids Farewell To Its Founder." *The National Forumeer*. August. 1.

[4]   See Avila, Alex. 1996. "Freedom Fighter." *Hispanic* magazine. (January–February): 20.

[5]   George, Ron. 1996. "Prominent Attend Vigil for Garcia," *Corpus Christi Caller-Times*. 30 July. A1.

[6]   *Ibid.*

[7]   Averyt, Libby. 1996. "Vaya Con Dios, Doctor." *Corpus Christi Caller-Times*. 31 July. A1.

[8]   Flores, David. 1996. "1,500 Mourn Founder of GI Forum." *San Antonio Express-News*. 30 July. 9A.

[9]   Barnes, Rosemary. 1996. "A Time To Say Goodbye." *Corpus Christi Caller-Times*. 30 July. A1.

[10]   Rivera, Anissa. 1996. "From Near and Far They Came, They Wept, They Remembered." *Corpus Christi Caller-Times*. 31 July. A 10.

Index